York Indep

Eastern Stage Bus ⸱perators

STUART EMMETT

KEY
Books

BRITAIN'S BUSES SERIES, VOLUME 2

Title page image: Gorwood OVF418 waits on St Denys Road, York. (Peter Yeomans, The Bus Archive)

Contents page image: Bailey HWF420E loading on Piccadilly, York. (Roy Marshall, The Bus Archive)

Published by Key Books
An imprint of Key Publishing Ltd
PO Box 100
Stamford
Lincs PE19 1XQ

www.keypublishing.com

The right of Stuart Emmett to be identified as the author of this book has been asserted in accordance with the Copyright, Designs and Patents Act 1988 Sections 77 and 78.

Copyright © Stuart Emmett, 2020

ISBN 978 1 913295 93 6

20 21 22 23 24 10 9 8 7 6 5 4 3 2 1

Typeset by SJmagic DESIGN SERVICES, India.

Contents

Author's Note

I hope you enjoy the journey through this book. It has been very pleasurable to research and write and could not have happened without the many wonderful photographers who recorded history for us. There are pictures from many sources, and I am so grateful to them all for their work, foresight and diligence over the years. I am especially grateful to them for sharing their work and not keeping images locked away.

Of course, it is not always possible to obtain perfect images of every bus operated, and those included in the book are used to present as complete a record as possible when alternative images could not be found. For me, the words are the easy part of a book, finding right images is the hardest part; but as my gravestone may well say, 'He tried'. Having said this, research never finishes as there are always some gaps. Therefore, if anyone can assist to fill in such gaps, then I would be delighted to hear from you.

The proceeds from the book sales, after deduction of costs, are going 100 per cent to assist bus preservation/archives. Indeed, many of the image providers and I have supplied our services free of charge to help this worthy initiative.

Unless stated below, the pictures are from my own collection, which is made up of our family pictures as well as those from other sources. For the latter, where the original photographer cannot be traced, I offer my apologies to them for the lack of accreditation and would be pleased to correct this in any future edition.

Images have been supplied by the following people, in no specific order: Roy Marshall, John Bennett, John Cockshott, John Sinclair, D. S. Giles, R. C. Davis, Peter Henson, David Hudson, Peter Yeomans, John Law and Mike Davies. The following image providers have also supplied images: Andrew Sefton, The Bus Archive, The Transport Library, Mineralcraft and PM Photography.

Introduction

All the operators in this book had similarities and typically, like many rural bus services, they started by running a service to their nearest market town. This was often done to get a second income with 'service' always being a strong point that supplemented their main living from farming and agriculture. Some bus services, such as Gorwood's (see Chapter 5), started out with horse carriages and then moved on to motor vehicles after the First World War.

All the operators were family based and often only some family members were involved. As time progressed, sons and nephews could enter the business that, by then, had commonly grown to offer excursions and private hires. The family side was both a strength and a weakness; families do not always see eye to eye and the death of a founding member could also bring about the end of the business.

However, what finally killed most of the operators in this book were changes to the way of life. Increased TV coverage in the 1950s meant visits to the cinema were no longer of interest, and the growth of car ownership meant buses were not the only means of travel. With economic changes in agriculture, combined with the growth of factory-based work, rural communities in turn changed and many became dormitory living places. Villages were therefore no longer places of work and employment. Accordingly, most of the supporting services of shops, doctors and schools collapsed and, along with them, many of the true country bus operators.

The magnet town for the area was the splendid city of York, whose history goes back to Roman times, and the Roman legacy still exists with the celebrated city walls. This traditional county town of Yorkshire bursts with historic attractions that today make it such a popular tourist destination.

At the confluence of the rivers Ouse and Foss, York lies on flat, arable land called the Vale of York, which is bordered to the west by the Pennines, to the northeast by the North York Moors and to the east by the rolling Yorkshire Wolds. All of these are lovely places, but then, as a Yorkshire man, I am biased as York is, for me, the best city in the UK.

In the 1800s, York became a railway hub and a confectionery-manufacturing centre (e.g. Rowntree's Kit-Kat and Terry's Chocolate Orange). Even as recently as the early 1980s, just five employers employed 30 per cent of the workforce and 75 per cent of manufacturing jobs were with just four companies. However, in recent decades, the economy of York has moved away from being dominated by these two sectors. Now the emphasis is on providing services, and the red brick university and health services sector are the major employers. Tourism remains an important element of the local economy along with new developments in the fields of science and technology.

Once out of the city and into the Vale of York, many beautiful small country villages are hidden away in the flat, fertile, agricultural arable land that dominates the area, and farms line the roads. This meant that York was a frontier town where many bus operators provided services, especially on market days. Consequently, routes were very rural, and besides catering for the traditional market day shoppers, they often carried a considerable volume of passengers to work in York. This remained the case until the car slowly became the preferred form of transport and so, today, York now has many Park & Ride bus schemes.

The many former rural services that linked the local towns and villages with York are most interesting operations. Historically, one large independent operator was York Pullman, which has been covered in another book, so this book will concentrate on the other stage bus companies that operated in the 1950s and 1960s from the east of York; the operators running into York from the west side will be covered in a future book.

Therefore, we look first at a large operator, Everingham of Pocklington, which was also the first one to finish in 1953. Also running into Pocklington was Bailey, who even coordinated timings on one route with Everingham. Both Everingham and Bailey ran from Stamford Bridge into York, where they met with Broadbent of Stamford Bridge. Bailey also ran north from Pocklington to Malton and so ran near to Milburn of Leavening. Finally, to the south of York and to the east of the River Ouse, Gorwood of East Cottingwith also ran at one time, alongside Everingham, into York.

Former Everingham coach with East Yorkshire.

Chapter 1

Everingham Brothers Ltd, Pocklington

(known as EB Motor Services)

Pocklington is a small market town at the foot of the Yorkshire Wolds in east Yorkshire. With a recent population of 8,337, it is 12.5 miles east of York and 22 miles northwest of Hull. It is known as the gateway to the Yorkshire Wolds, an area of many low hills and steep valleys underlain by chalk. This unusual topography results in an 'upside-down' farming system with livestock (mostly sheep and cows) grazing in the valleys and the hills above being used for crops. Therefore, most of the valleys exist in open space and are not former river valleys, indeed surface water is a rare sight in the Wolds.

The Wolds make an arc from the Humber Estuary, west of Hull, up to the North Sea coast between Bridlington and Scarborough. Here, they rise up to form cliffs, most notably at Flamborough, Bempton and Filey. A national footpath, the Wolds Way, passes close to Pocklington at Millington in the central Wolds. During the Second World War, the relative flatness of the area was used to build airfields near to Pocklington and these included Full Sutton, Melbourne, Elvington, Rufforth, Driffield and Holme-on-Spalding-Moor, with Pocklington's own airfield opening in June 1941.

Traditionally, Pocklington was heavily involved in agriculture along with trades like ropemaking, brickmaking and brewing. There were also corn mills, iron foundries and the production of agricultural implements. Indeed, John Thomas Everingham was a master tailor with three shops and had three sons and a stepson. The two youngest brothers were Sidney and Irwin who, whilst not starting bus operations until after the First World War, liked motorcycles and so opened a dealership in 1904. They also went on to operate a landaulette (the word is a derivative of a landau horse-drawn carriage) with an open driver's seat, an enclosed rear section with one cross seat and a collapsible roof.

Plans for a taxi service came into fruition and thoughts were given to a haulage service and a funeral business. However, the outbreak of the First World War stopped this and whilst his brothers left to serve, Irwin was not accepted because of health reasons and assisted his father in the tailoring business.

EVERINGHAM Bros.
MOTOR ENGINEERS,
RAILWAY STREET, POCKLINGTON,
AGENTS for all the Leading Makes of MOTOR CARS, MOTOR CYCLES, and ordinary BICYCLES.

Motor Landaulette
FOR HIRE
on
Reasonable Terms.

ACCESSORIES. REPAIRS by Skilled Workmen.

Outside the garage on Railway Street, fleet number 1 was purchased second-hand in 1921. It was a 1916 Daimler with an unknown body, recorded as B32F, but it also has a rear entrance, therefore is B32R or B32D. It was kept until 1927. (The Bus Archive)

In 1919, soon after the war had ended, the brothers bought two former military vehicles, and these were used on haulage and passenger services; the first motor services being on 11 February 1919.

Haulage runs were sometimes more than 200 miles, with round trips to Liverpool carrying farm produce and then back via Huddersfield to collect coal. Livestock, including sheep, were also a regular part of their work. Demountable charabanc bodies were fitted for weekend excursions that ran to Bridlington and Scarborough, round trips of about 60 and 70 miles respectively. These proved popular, for example:

> In the summertime there are pleasure trips to the seaside resorts organised by Everingham Bros, and these are very much enjoyed, for the passengers are conveyed at a very reasonable price, by big saloons which have every comfort for long journeys.

A market day service to York was requested, so in February 1920 (also reported as 1921), Everingham operated a route once a week. However, York only licensed EB for three buses in October 1922, so if they ran before then, they would have used private land for their York terminus (such as a pub). Additional second-hand vehicles were bought in 1921 and 1922, some only for passengers and some with truck/passenger demountable bodies.

Furniture removals were started and the Pocklington to York market day service soon became daily. Therefore, by 1923, three routes to York were to form the backbone of Everingham's bus business and these were as follows:

- A direct route of around 13 miles on the A1079 via Wilberfoss.
- The northern route, around 21 miles, to the A166 via Yapham, Bishop Wilton and Stamford Bridge.
- The southern route, the longest at around 24 miles, which meandered to the east of the Pocklington Canal, going to Beilby, Everingham (the village), Seaton Ross and Melbourne before joining the B1228 to go over the canal at Hagg Bridge to Sutton upon Derwent and Elvington.

EB15 is a 1927 Dennis with a Barnaby B32F body. It is shown loading in York for the southern Pocklington route via Melbourne. The luggage roof rack is holding a large market basket. After withdrawal, it was sold to a Mr Watson in Seaton Ross for conversion to a lorry. (The Bus Archive)

The success of the three York routes was noticeable and reported as quickly going from the initial twice weekly service to operating daily. Then, in 1925, the headways were said to be every two hours and then every hour. Also, in 1926, the direct route was reported as running every 30 minutes. However, with the northern route there is no evidence of even a daily operation before 1928. Further research is needed to establish what actually happened.

The increase in services prompted a thankful villager on the southern route to note: 'This bus is a great advantage to Seaton Ross, for we villagers are able to go to town and to market whenever we wish. It is often thought how lucky we are to possess such a good bus service, considering that Seaton Ross is such a small village.'

In 1926, services were boosted by the closure to passengers of the Derwent Valley Light Railway, a 16-mile line that ran from Layerthorpe in York to Cliffe Common, near Selby.

An all-1926 Leyland, fleet number 12, that was later reported in 1946 as being with the Bronte Bus Company in Haworth. Market Weighton is on the destination. This Saturday-only route started in 1924 but was reported closed by 1926, others however say it was still running in 1928.

In 1928, a service from York to Bridlington was started. This was a long route of 42 miles operating from York on the direct route to Pocklington and then via Huggate, Warter, North Dalton, Kirkham, Driffield, Nafferton, Burton Agnes and Carnaby.

Growth in Everingham's bus network continued from Pocklington, with new routes being added in 1929. The new routes were a circular from Pocklington via Nunburnholme and Burnby and one from Pocklington via Allerthorpe to Melbourne; this was at some time extended by around nine miles to Bubwith and Howden as a trial, but the extension was later ended.

As we will soon see, new vehicles now came thick and fast with AECs and Thornycrofts, the latter with Barnaby of Hull bodies. Saturday-only services also now ran to the nearby village of Millington and there was also an 8-mile route via Warter to Huggate; the latter was also extended to Driffield once a day on Tuesdays, Thursdays and Saturdays.

These shorter routes from Pocklington were designed as feeders to connect Pocklington to EB's York routes. In total, EB served just over 50 villages in an essentially rural area, where on most routes a single vehicle was all that was needed. An exception was the Bridlington route in the summer, when it was often duplicated. On other routes, at weekends, the 20-seater buses were replaced by 32 seaters, leaving the 20 seaters to run on the Saturday-only routes to Millington and Huggate. Peak-hour traffic in and out of York, largely consisting of the Rowntree factory workers, was usually covered by an extra service or by running duplicates.

Also in 1929, a regular service ran every hour from York to Heslington, a short 15-minute journey. An 18-minute journey from York via Dunnington to Four Lane Ends near Kexby was also run.

May 1925 brought BT8468, maybe fleet number 8, a Thornycroft A1 with a Barnaby B20F body. Everingham used such small buses on the light-traffic routes and narrow roads.

1944 Bedford OWB51 loads on Piccadilly York for the short 15-minute run to Heslington that ran almost every hour and was interworked with the 18-minute route to Dunnington/Kexby. (The Bus Archive)

In the early 1930s, the haulage services were dropped but an extensive parcels service using the buses was still operated. This sometimes ran on the York market days and was a goods vehicle 'duplicate' used to carry the large quantities of produce for sale, including such items as rabbits, eggs, vegetables and flowers.

On the 27 March 1933, the company was registered with three shareholders as Everingham Brothers Limited, with capital of £8,000 and a registered office at 10 Railway Street, Pocklington. In 1937, *Motor Transport* reported a fleet of 34 vehicles, including two motor hearses and an ambulance.

In 1934, bus 30 arrived. This was a milestone as it was the first AEC Regal/Barnaby-bodied bus. In total, Everingham bought 12 by 1950. 30 is parked in Pocklington. (The Bus Archive)

Excursions had been started from Pocklington and private hires were operated, for example for the staff of Barnaby coachbuilders in Hull, the body provider of choice for Everingham between the mid-20s and 1952. Suggestions were available for private hires and these included destinations like Aysgarth Falls, Hawes, Richmond, Ambleside, Windermere, Redcar, Whitby, Matlock and Chatsworth. Additionally, EB had licences for a service from Pocklington to Barmby Moor Institute and from York to the racecourse (York Pullman also had such a licence). Many dance and football specials were also run, including to the pantomime in Leeds. School work was also undertaken.

During the Second World War, military work was undertaken for the nearby aerodromes at Elvington, Pocklington, Melbourne and Full Sutton. Additionally, the buses also often carried retailers' deliveries that had previously been sent via van and these included groceries, meat and laundry. EB had, at the time, 52 parcels agents within its area of operations.

In 1945, a forced step change came when Sidney Everingham died, leaving control with Irwin, who was still not a healthy man. However, fleet renewal continued and from then until 1953 came six single deckers, two AEC coaches, two Commer coaches, two double deckers and two rebodied double deckers.

However, in 1952 Irwin decided to sell and so in November 1953, EB, including 31 vehicles, passed over to East Yorkshire Motor Services (EYMS) for £29,000. Sixteen vehicles entered service with EYMS and 15 were sold to a dealer in January 1954. The depots remained in Pocklington and were replaced by a new one built by EYMS that opened on 1 May 1956.

WF1234 was a Leyland LSC3 with a Leyland body from 1928 and numbered 18. It is involved in a large children's excursion, with watching crowds, organised by the York Poor Children's Fresh Air Fund around 1934. This excursion had also used at least three other operators – Broadbent, West Yorkshire Road Car, and Corcoran of Tadcaster – and had been organised since the early 1900s (this run is referred to again in the Broadbent section of this book).

The Railway Station and Station Road in Pocklington with the EB depot to the left and at least four buses parked. 35, WF9035, is a 1936 Albion with a Barnaby 20-seater body that was used on narrow lanes. Alongside, is 58 from 1950, an AEC Regal with a 35-seater Barnaby body. (The Bus Archive)

Piccadilly in York and, in the distance, a Bedford OWB that looks like one of the two belonging to EB that came in late 1942/early 1943, numbered 47/48. This picture has other bus connections. The owner of Foxton's Garage, one Hartas Foxton, kept his red bus vehicles, which ran to Linton, Helperby and Easingwold, there. This operation, run with Norman Pearce, formed the York Pullman Bus Company Limited in October 1926 and that story is told in another book by the author.

Also visible, to the left of the OWB, is the iron foundry of William Dove and Sons Ltd. This building features often in Chapter 2 as Bailey's York terminus was outside the premises, just behind the Bedford OWB.

Routes

This is largely based on the 1948 timetable.

Timetable service number	From/to	Maximum days of operating	Maximum journeys a day	Journey time	Comments and possible start date
1	Pocklington, Wilberfoss to York	Daily	23	38 mins	Direct route 1921/2
2	Pocklington, Bielby, Everingham, Seaton Ross, Melbourne, Hagg Bridge, Sutton, Elvington to York	Daily	9	65 mins to York, return 70 mins	Southern route 1921/2
3*	Pocklington, Yapham, Bishop Wilton, Bugthorpe, Stamford Bridge to York	Daily	5	75 mins	Northern route 1921/2
4	York, Dunnington to Kexby Crossing	Daily	8 (plus 1 extended to Rowntree's)	18 mins (28 mins)	York licensed in June 1929 to Dunnington
5	York to Heslington	Daily	9 plus 2 on Saturday	15 mins	York licensed in June 1929
6	York, Wilberfoss, Pocklington, Huggate, Warter, North Dalton, Kirkburn, Driffield, Nafferton, Burton Agnes to Bridlington	Daily	6	1 hour 58 mins	1928 A crew was based at Bridlington
7	Pocklington to Millington	Saturday only	3	15 mins	By 1929
8	Pocklington, Warter to Huggate	Saturday only	3	28 mins	By 1929
9	Pocklington, Allerthorpe, Melbourne, East Cottingham, Bubwith, Spaldington to Howden	Daily Saturday Sunday	4 journeys 5 journeys 2 journeys	70 mins	By 1934 and stopped in the late 1940s
10	Pocklington, Kilnwick Gates, Nunburnholme, Burnby, Hayton, back to Pocklington	Daily	1 journey clockwise and 1 anti-clockwise	33/35 mins	By 1929
10	Pocklington, Burnby, Nunburnholme, Kilnwick Double Gates to Pocklington	Wednesday and Saturday only	2 journeys 5 journeys	30 mins	By 1929

Timetable service number	From/to	Maximum days of operating	Maximum journeys a day	Journey time	Comments and possible start date
11	Pocklington, Allerthorpe, Melbourne, East Cottingham, Hagg Bridge, Sutton, Elvington to York	Monday to Saturday	1 journey	75 mins out and 70 mins back	By 1929
12	Pocklington, Warter, Huggate, Tibthorpe to Driffield	Tuesday/ Thursday and Saturday	1 journey	60 mins	By 1929

* The northern route 3 to York was for many years exactly the same as the Bailey Bus Service one from Fangfoss. This is fully commented on in Chapter 2.

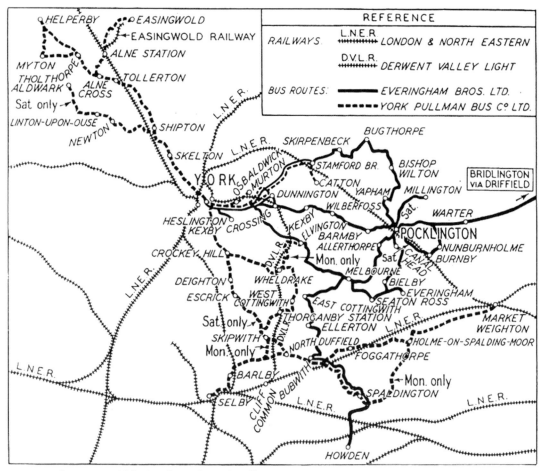

Route map from 1941 which also shows the York Pullman routes.

With the takeover by East Yorkshire Motor Services in November 1953, route changes were inevitable as East Yorkshire already had long-distance services that passed through Everingham's operating area. These were three services from Leeds, all joint with West Yorkshire Road Car. Route 10 went via York to Hull via Pocklington, with seven daily journeys, and the other two services went to Bridlington; the 26 via Pocklington and the 25 via Stamford Bridge, with a maximum of 11 journeys and three journeys, respectively.

The initial changes made by East Yorkshire to the routes were as follows:

Route numbers EB/EY	Destination	Daily maximum journeys	Comments
1/ 54	York direct	Same as EB, along with the existing EY10 and 26 routes	Diverted by Dunnington to replace EB4
2/ 55	York via Melbourne	Reduced from 9 to 5	New shorts from Pocklington to East Cottingwith and York to Melbourne
3/ 56	York via Bishop Wilton	Stayed the same	Bailey 'competed' on this route
4	York to Dunnington/ Kexby	Withdrawn	Replaced by the diversion of route 54
5	York to Heslington	Same but now operated by York-West Yorkshire	Replaced by York-West Yorkshire route 17
6/ (25/26)	York to Bridlington	Incorporated into existing EY routes	Replaced by EY25 and 26
7/ 57	Millington	Stayed the same	
8/ 58	Huggate	Stayed the same	
9/ 62	Howden	Stayed the same	
10/ 59	Pocklington Circular	Stayed the same	
11/ 60	York via East Cottingham	Stayed the same	
12/ 61	Driffield	Stayed the same	

East Yorkshire gradually made changes, and this included, for example, giving up route 56 in 1958, when Bailey took up some of the timings. Meanwhile, the East Yorkshire timetable map opposite shows these former Everingham routes.

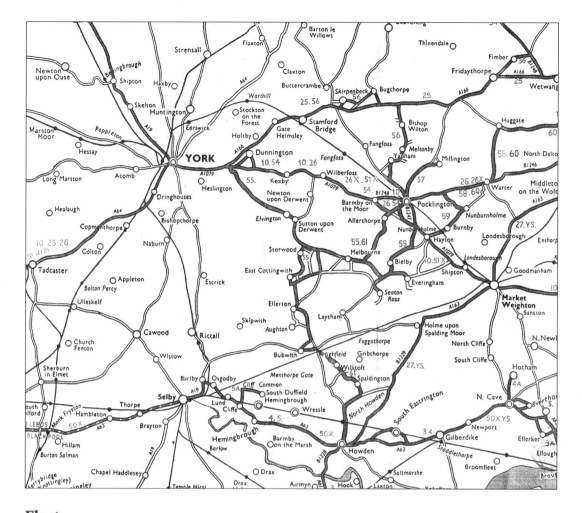

Fleet

Everingham became a regular buyer of AECs from 1929, and they used mainly Commers, Bedfords and Albions for smaller buses. In 1939, each bus ran about 50/55,000 miles per year and, overall, the fleet did around 700,000 miles and carried around 700,000 passengers each year. Two mechanics and two cleaners worked nights and in 1939 a total of 42 people were employed.

During the Second World War, nine vehicles entered the fleet between 1940 and 1945. These were Leylands, Bedford OWBs and Daimler utility double deckers, the latter being clearly to service the large local military requirements.

From 1947, it was fully back to AECs with, of course, Barnaby bodies. A specified feature on the single deckers was a small box on the top of the destination box with the initials 'EB'. This 'EB box' was reported to 'distinguish themselves by having EB placed in a prominent position in the front of the bus. During wintertime, these letters are illuminated so as to cause no hesitation as to whether the passengers are stopping the right bus or not'. Indeed, on the eventual sale to East Yorkshire, a newspaper headline read, 'Folk will miss the EB sign', and continued with, 'The familiar EB sign has come to mean friendship to country people and its passing will be received with regret and a feeling that that an old friend has passed on'.

Garages in Pocklington

Everingham was said to have used three garages in Pocklington:

- Red House Barn, in Pocklington. This was at Red House Farm on Yapham Road at the junction with Garths End. It was the first 'depot' with room for two/three vehicles. The farm was, however, partially destroyed when an RAF heavy bomber crashed into the farmhouse during the war.
- Railway Street. However, 10 and 12 Railway Street was actually the loading point and also where the EB office was. The depot was just around the corner on Station Road and was known as 'Station Garage'; it opened in 1921 and had a large yard and maintenance facilities.
- Flacks Yard or Flax Yard. Everingham used one of the yards but it is not known which. The first was a former vets premises with stables at an unknown location, and the other was where a flax mill had burnt down in 1856 at the corner of Market Street, Chapmangate and Hallgate on the B1246 to Warter.

The depot on Station Road, overlooking the railway station. Railway Street is on the left of where the photographer is stood.

Livery

The livery was light grey and white with steel blue bands and a varied name/logo style. 'Grey Saloons' was used in the company's advertising. The letter heading below gives an indication of the shades of blue and shows one style of logo.

The logo varied and the following styles have been noted:

- The above garter logo seems to have been used until the mid-1930s but with white, not blue, lettering within a steel blue-coloured circle.
- The name in script over the garter was used before the Second World War, from around 1937.
- Script only was used post-war, by 1948.
- A circle and horizontal lines were used from 1950.

Fleet Details

In a former life with Yorkshire Woollen District at Shepley Bridge, near Mirfield, is C7577. This Daimler is thought to have been new in 1913 and is seen here with a later body. It was with Everingham, possibly as fleet number 3, from April 1921 until June 1922, when it went to F&H Croft in Yeadon, near Leeds.

Number 9, HO6349, in a superb quality image taken by the chassis builders, Thornycroft, sporting a Wilton Carriage Works dual-door body. New in October 1924 and used as a demonstrator, it came to Everingham in September 1925 and had a rear-entrance body. It was next used by someone in Hull in 1929, fitted with a freight-carrying body. (The Bus Archive)

Number 19, WF1550, new in August 1928, was a Thorneycroft A6 with a Barnaby 20-seater body. It is shown on the southern route to York via Melbourne and is perhaps in Elvington.

WF4886, numbered 26, was new in 1932 and is a Maudslay ML6/Barnaby complete with rear roof rack.

WF5058, numbered 27, is also from 1932 and is a Bedford WLB with a 20-seater Barnaby body.

WF5628, numbered 28, was a 1933 Albion Victor with a Barnaby body. Number 28 stayed until 1949 at North Bay in Scarborough. (The Bus Archive)

A nearside view of WF6830, numbered 30, their first AEC Regal, complete with rear roof rack. An AEC Regal with a Barnaby body, it was withdrawn in September 1950. (The Bus Archive)

WF7632, numbered 32, was an Albion/Barnaby from 1935 and had a ten-year life. It looks to be with 28, shown on page 21. (The Bus Archive)

The front single decker is 34, WF8834, an AEC Regal with a Barnaby body which was new in April 1937 and with EB until the end in 1953. There is an unconfirmed report that this bus was rebodied in 1950. 34 was not used by EYMS. However, it was used by a showman. The double decker behind is 36 and is shown on page 31.

No images of 36, WF9936, have been found from when it was with Everingham, but here it is with its second owner, Wilson & Hughes, trading as White Bus in Bridlington. New in April 1937, it was a rare Dodge RB with the usual Barnaby body. It did ten years with Everingham before going to White Bus and was withdrawn in September 1950 before being scrapped in 1951. (The Bus Archive)

Seen here registered as AWF137, 37 from 1937, an AEC Regal with a Barnaby body is by the parish church of St James at Warter, to the east of Pocklington on the Bridlington route. This was a posed picture that appeared in the *AEC Gazette* in April 1939. When compared with the next picture, this becomes a mystery bus and was said to be later registered as ABT137. However, the body shown above is a Barnaby standard pre-war body, and the body in the next picture is the Barnaby post-war body. It is, however, believed the above picture was faked for PR purposes and is actually AWF541, fleet no 41, so the registration AWF137 was, therefore, faked. (The Bus Archive)

Fleet number 37 again, but now as ABT137. The body here is clearly the six-bay post-war Barnaby body, yet there is no report of it being rebodied, although intriguingly, 40 (AWF540) was said to have been rebodied in 1948 after the original body was burnt out. However, no picture has been found of 40. Therefore, currently, it is believed 37 was always ABT137 and it was this bus and not 40 that was rebodied post war.

Numbers 38 and 39, registered AWF38 and AWF39, which were Bedford WTBs with Barnaby B20F bodies, came in January 1938. 38 is on Station Road, with the depot in the background, alongside the building that was used at one time as a clothing factory to support Everingham's tailor's shop, which was just round the corner on the left in Railway Street.

40 and 41 (above) were further AEC Regals with Barnaby bodies and came in May 1938. This picture is another picture used in the April 1939 *AEC Gazette* article and was posed, though perhaps the man of the right with bike clips was roped in as he was passing?

BWF944 came in May 1940 and was the last AEC Regal/Barnaby until 1947. The engine cover on 44 looks different from the earlier ones. There is also no Autovac, as were found on the post-war bodies.

BWF945 from August 1940, when 45 entered service. It was a Leyland TS8 and an unusual purchase, perhaps because of wartime influences, but it did have the normal Barnaby body. The lower radiator cover is tied with string, which was definitely a DIY job! The picture is said to have been taken at Keeling/Heavy Motor Services in Leeds after it was sold on by EYMS in November 1953. Keeling ran buses on contract and was also a haulage operator, indeed they converted buses into trucks.

Here in Piccadilly, York, is 46 CWF46, bought in May 1942. This, Everingham's first double decker, was a Leyland TD7 with an NCME utility L53R body.

Next were 47 and 48, the two Bedford OWBs mentioned earlier. 49 was registered as JP5049 by the bodybuilder Massey, and this Daimler CWG5 came in July 1943 with a utility H56R body for which no pictures were found. 49 was, however, rebodied and is seen here at York on Piccadilly, after 1952, with its new Barnaby H56R body. Just behind the bus can be seen the lettering for the William Dove and Sons Ltd iron foundry, which also features in Chapter 2 of this book. (The Bus Archive)

Daimler CWA6 50 came in January 1944 with a Duple utility H56R body. No pictures have been found of this bus either. However, like 49, it was rebodied in 1952 by Barnaby and is seen below, probably in Pocklington near to the depot. (The Bus Archive)

July 1944 brought another Bedford OWB/Duple, DBT51, which was numbered 51. This eventually had an 'EB box' fitted on top of the standard utility-style destination screen. This picture was taken on 19 April 1954, and 51 was sold to a dealer or a farmer in Hornsea in August 1954. Interestingly, 51 was reported last registered in October 1961 but exactly what it was doing in the intervening years is a mystery. (John Cockshott)

Another wartime acquisition, 52, DBT152, was bought in July 1944. A Daimler CWA6 with a Northern Counties utility H56R body, it was not operated by East Yorkshire but was scrapped in 1954.

A view of Pocklington, looking towards Railway Street. To the right, behind the two cyclists, is Station Road where the EB bus depot was. Everingham services started just to right, on Railway Street, and the bus shown, 53, the 1944 Daimler/Duple utility, is turning towards there. Subsequently, new buildings came to the corner behind the bus and also down the left side of Railway Street.

Purchased in April 1944, 53 was the last wartime buy and was another Daimler CWA6 but this time with a Duple UH56R body. It was numbered 53 and was registered as DBT553.

53 was taken into the East Yorkshire fleet as their 653 and ran in service until December 1956, when it was transferred to the ancillary fleet. It then became a left-luggage store and office in Westwood bus station in Scarborough until November 1968, after which it was scrapped.

54 and 55 were the first post-war deliveries in April and May 1947, respectively. The AEC Regal/Barnaby connection remained, and this post-war body now had six bays, not seven as on the pre-war version. In the absence of an image of 54 with EB, the photograph above shows it when it was with East Yorkshire, where it stayed until December 1956 before undergoing a metamorphosis.

654 was reborn in December 1956 as a recovery vehicle and is parked up on the Market Place in Beverley. It was kept until March 1968 when it was scrapped.

55 is parked outside the EB offices on Railway Street, Pocklington, and is alongside EB60. All the immediate walled area behind was subsequently built on.

55 became EY655 and was withdrawn in June 1955 and sold in March 1956. 655 was last traced to Lane Bros in Mansfield in July 1959.

It seems EB had a liking for double deckers as in July 1948, 36 came in with a registration number of JX2037. New in 1934 to Halifax CT, it was an AEC Regent with an English Electric H54R body. Not operated by East Yorkshire, it seems to have ended up with a showman. (The Bus Archive)

GWF256, numbered 56, was a new AEC Regent III with a Barnaby H56R body. It is shown here in January 1949. 56 went on to become EY656.

57, HBT457, here on the York Racecourse specials, was yet another AEC Regal/Barnaby and entered service in July 1949. It was to become EY657.

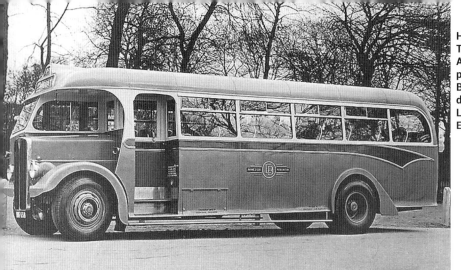

HWF658 in May 1950. This was another AEC Regal/Barnaby, probably posed by Barnaby. The porch door is clearly seen. Later, 58 would become EY658.

May 1950 also brought in 59, HWF659, which was originally intended for West Bridgford Urban District Council. Another AEC Regal, but with a Harrington body, this was destined to become EY659. (The Bus Archive)

JBT160 was the last AEC Regal/Barnaby in July 1950 and 60 is parked outside the EB offices on Railway Street on the direct run to York. It would become EY660 and was withdrawn in March 1963 when it joined EY659 with a contractor in Birmingham in April 1963.

Not the best image of KWF761 but a historic one as 61 and 62 were the last new buses purchased by Everingham. They were AEC Regal IVs with rare Barnaby C37C bodies and delivered in September 1952. They became EY661/662.

The rear end of 61 as EY661 at Bridlington alongside a coach from Fred Knowles of Oulton, near Leeds. Both EY661/662 had a normal life with East Yorkshire and stayed in service until September 1965 and were both last noted with Miller, a contractor who bought them in September 1966. (John Sinclair)

The last buys by Everingham were CVN240/241, ex-Wallace Arnold 1946 Commer/Plaxton coaches that had been based in Scarborough and bought in October 1952 at the end of the summer season in Scarborough. These passed over to East Yorkshire who sold them on to Hedon Motor Coaches in December 1953. They ran them until October 1959 and March 1962, with 241 going to Watson in Bridlington for a year. Whilst no images were found of the two Commers with EB, three of them, along with two half-cab coaches and a Bedford OB, are shown outside the Wallace Arnold Columbus Ravine depot in Scarborough.

Chapter 2

Baileys, Fangfoss

(trading as Bailey Bus Service)

Bailey's pre-story starts with the marriage in 1901 of John Townsley Bailey to his wife, Jemima. John and Jemima were from local villages and at the time of their marriage John was a joiner and wheelwright in his father's business at Bishop Wilton. He went on to become a joiner at the North Eastern Railway carriage works.

In 1903, they started a family with the birth of Chrissie, followed in 1904 by John, then Phyllis in 1908, Marjorie in 1909 and Denis in 1919. John, Marjorie and Denis are the Baileys that feature in this evolving story.

John Bailey (the younger) eventually lived in Bolton, a village on the road between Fangfoss and Pocklington. In the early 1920s, possibly 1924, he bought a Ford Model T 14-seater in Manchester and ran it on Saturdays between Fangfoss and York, a distance of just over 13 miles. He also developed a haulage business, and indeed later, former bus bodies were known to be used as stores and their chassis as wagons.

Nearby, three miles away in Bishop Wilton, a Mr Jackson bought a similar bus and it also ran to York on a Saturday as well to the Thursday market. However, this bus burnt out so John Bailey started to run the service and bought another Model T from the Leeds and Tadcaster Omnibus Company. Later, a local joiner built a body on a Ford 1-ton truck chassis.

York gave licences for the following routes:

- York to Bishop Wilton, in March 1927. Three daily journeys ran, increasing to four on a Monday (with an earlier journey) and also to four on Thursdays (with a later one on York market day).
- York to Stamford Bridge, in September 1928. There were five journeys on a Saturday with extensions of three journeys going to Yapham via Bugthorpe, Skirpenbeck and Bishop Wilton and two journeys going to Bishop Wilton, missing out Skirpenbeck.

Also advertised at this time was a 'Saturday Goods Service'. This was especially for taking market produce from Bishop Wilton to York via Youlthorpe, Gowthorpe, Fangfoss and Bolton. Additionally, three runs went from Bolton, Fangfoss, Full Sutton, Brick Yards and Stamford Bridge; these journeys arrived in York at 0955, 1355 and 2025 hours and left at 1200, 1700 and 2100 hours, respectively.

It is thought that before the Road Traffic Act changes in September 1930 all the necessary licences for bus operations had been granted by York Council and were for eight buses.

After the Model T Fords, four-cylinder Chevrolets were the next purchases with most having bodies built by Allen of Brigg. General Motors purchased Chevrolet and in 1931 the new Bedford WLB chassis appeared. This became Bailey's standard bus, and whilst other makes were purchased, Bedfords were the bus of choice into the 1970s. Indeed, in the 1950s and early 1960s, Bailey's country stage bus routes were Bedford OB heaven!

The Bedford OB has a special place in bus history. It succeeded the Bedford WTB in 1939 and just 73 were built before the Second World War stopped production. In 1942, the Ministry of War Transport selected Bedford as the supplier of single deckers to essential users and thus was born the OWB. The same mechanically as the OB, it was built using cheaper and more readily available materials such as cast iron. The bodies were basic, and the design used straight, rather than rounded, panels along with wooden slatted seats. Around 3,800 OWBs were built before post-war production started, and that number went up to 12,700 by the time production stopped in 1951. Whilst some 5,500 of these were exported, it still meant that there were few places in the UK that did not use the OB. As a small bus (it was 24ft 4ins long and 7ft 6ins wide), it was ideal in rural country areas. As we will see, many ran in such regions for decades.

VY2555 was a Chevrolet LQ from 1931.

VY2755 was another 1931 Chevrolet LQ with an unknown body. Driver, Percy Hopper, is on the steps of the 14-seater. (Andrew Sefton)

Bishop Wilton church can be seen in the background of WF4569, a Bedford WLB from late 1931/early 1932 with an unknown 20-seater body. (Andrew Sefton)

CHL679 is a typical Bedford OB with a Duple Vista body, this one from 1950, and was with Bailey between 1955 and 1967. Bailey accumulated 13 Bedford OWB/OBs from 1947 and in the 1950s there were between five and nine in service at any one time. Their last OB was withdrawn in 1968. (PM Photography)

Routes

From	Via	Days of operating	Maximum return journeys a day	Journey time	Comments
Bugthorpe (Church Corner) to York (Piccadilly)	Barthorpe, Acklam, Leppington, Gally Gap, Howsham, Harton and the A64	Thursday and Saturday	1	?	Withdrawn September 1960
Bugthorpe	Kirby Underdale	Thursday	?	?	?
Pocklington to Malton*	Southwold, Painsthorpe Top, Bugthorpe (from Malton only), Wold House, Thixendale Crossroads and Langton Lanes.	Saturday only	3 (Pocklington to Malton)	1 hour 15 mins	Malton to Pocklington, did a double run from Painsthorpe to Bugthorpe. Withdrawn June 1951
			3 (Malton to Pocklington)	1 hour 55 mins	
Pocklington to Malton** After Jan 1969 this ran only from Pocklington to Stamford Bridge	Bolton, Fangfoss, Full Sutton, Stamford Bridge, Buttercrambe Bridge, Gally Gap, Westow and Langton Lanes. Bolton, Fangfoss and Full Sutton	Monday–Friday Saturday Sunday Monday–Friday Saturday	4 7 3 3 4	1 hour 25 mins 30 mins	Stamford Bridge to Malton was withdrawn on Sundays in Sept 1955 Withdrawn on Monday to Saturday on 8/1/69
Pocklington to York + ++	Yapham, Meltonby, Bishop Wilton, Bugthorpe, Skirpenbeck, Stamford Bridge and Gate Helmsley	Monday–Friday Saturday Sunday	5 9 3	1 hour 15 mins	Sold to Ingleby on 13/5/85

 * All the southbound buses had connections at Bugthorpe. For example, the morning one at 1040 hours connected with the Pocklington/Bishop Wilton to York bus and the two evening journeys connected with the York to Pocklington service via Bishop Wilton at Bugthorpe at 1715 and 2115 hours.

** Short workings operated, for example, between Pocklington and Fangfoss two or three times a day and from Fangfoss to Stamford Bridge twice a day; some of these were likely bus depot positioning journeys.

 + Short workings operated, for example, between Bishop Wilton and York twice a day on Mondays and Thursdays only.

++ This route was identical to Everingham's route 3, even down to most of the timings and departure times. For example, at 10 past the hour from Pocklington BBS had six round trips and EB five round trips on Monday to Friday. The alternative timings approach was probably because of Traffic Commissioners' actions after 1930, coordinating the routes run by EB and Bailey. A Bishop Wilton resident recalls, 'there was a bus every hour, one to Pocklington and one to York. On the half hour there would often be two buses on the bridge facing opposite directions!' Bailey and Everingham were indeed timed to pass in Bishop Wilton. The route was certainly not jointly run and it is doubted that each accepted the other operators' tickets.

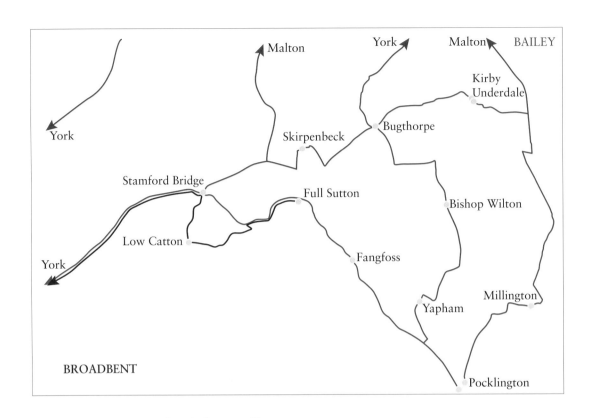

Bailey's Bedford OB GFU857 in typical countryside.

Stamford Bridge was, in today's language, a hub for Bailey. The services were arranged to connect as shown in the following example:

Arriving at 1255/1300 hours at Stamford Bridge were the following routes:

- Ex-Malton at 1200 hours, bound for Pocklington (via Fangfoss).
- Ex-Pocklington at 1230 hours (via Fangfoss), bound for Malton.
- Ex-York at 1230 hours (via Bishop Wilton), bound for Pocklington.
- Ex-Stamford Bridge at 1300 hours, bound for York (at one time Bailey had operated a bus running four shorts a day from Stamford Bridge to York).

This caused rivalry with Everingham Brothers and York Pullman on the route from between Stamford Bridge and York. At the resultant Traffic Commissioners meeting in 1936, they complained that Bailey was incorrectly using Stamford Bridge as a hub to connect the Pocklington to Malton route and the Pocklington to York service. This was upheld and all operators were required to re-align their timings and Bailey was stopped from running the shorts from Stamford Bridge to York.

However, the other 'natural and existing' connections at Stamford Bridge remained. These connections were the routes from Pocklington and Fangfoss to Stamford Bridge (which ran on to Malton until 1969) and the service from Pocklington via Bishop Wilton and Stamford Bridge to York.

During the Second World War, Bailey does not seem to have gained any military work from the many airbases built in the area. However, in 1946 they did apply for a stage service from RAF Full Sutton to Fangfoss railway station, which appears not to have been granted. They also moved from Bolton to Fangfoss in May 1946 and established a depot behind the Carpenters Arms pub; houses were subsequently built on the land.

In 1954, Bailey also applied for the Everingham Brothers' Pocklington to York via Bishop Wilton service that East Yorkshire had taken over in November 1953. This identical route with EB had coordinated timings and was retained by East Yorkshire as their route 56. However, on 5 July 1958, EY withdrew and the following day Bailey, finally, ran some of the timings.

The next major event was in January 1961, when John Bailey died at the age of 56, and the company passed over to family members. It was probably initially run by his sister, Marjorie, who had worked with John as a clerk. In April 1965, the company became Baileys Transport Limited.

Bus services were now in decline as car ownership increased, population decreased with migration to the cities and social habits became more home-based following growth in TV transmissions. The Pocklington to York service via Bishop Wilton was, therefore, reduced to four times a day and a fleet of six vehicles.

Parked at the depot are two buses that were together in the Bailey fleet between June 1965 and January 1966. The photographer thought that it was not the best picture, but I do like the atmospheric dust, and it is also of historical significance as it shows the Fangfoss depot well. (John Sinclair)

By August 1975, the owner was Denis Bailey, the younger brother who had worked as a tractor salesman. He was reported to have a tax claim of £4,642. Mr Bailey had understood payment by instalments had been agreed but had received a demand for full payment. He sought the assistance of the local press noting that, 'I shall have to offer them a bus and that means we won't be able to keep the bus service going'.

Ten years later, the company was sold to Ingleby's Luxury Coaches of York in May 1985 and Bailey's four remaining buses were passed over. Over 35 years later, some drivers' names are still remembered: Norman Parker from Bishop Wilton, known as 'Sparks'; Tate Kendra from Bolton; and Walter Brent from Fangfoss. A wartime evacuee stayed with the Brent family in Fangfoss and is on record as saying:

> Mr Brent, Auntie Vera's husband, used to drive Bailey's buses – everyone was very fond of him because Bailey's used to cross with Everingham's which was a Pocklington company, but everybody went on the Baileys buses. They started first and finished last, half past seven in the morning to York, and the last bus was half past nine at night back. Every two hours in the day to Pocklington, and the Everingham buses ran alternately with them.

Ingleby had been founded in May 1968 by Mr Chris Ingleby and initially had a Ford Transit minibus. In 1972, the first full-sized coach was purchased, and the trading name changed to Ingleby's Luxury Coaches. Five years later, they moved to Hospital Fields Road, Fulford Industrial Estate, in York, and they in turn were eventually bought by K&J Logistics, the new owner of the York Pullman brand, in 2007; but that's another story.

Subsequently, following bus deregulation, all the Bailey routes faded away and today all that is left in 2020 are two subsidised journeys a day from Pocklington via Bishop Wilton into York.

Bailey's Operating Environment

To give indications of the Bailey's operating environment, this section will look at some of the buses at work; full details of the buses follow after that.

JXE60 laying over in Malton before the delightful, 1 hour 25 mins, scenic trip back to Pocklington. (Roy Marshall)

Two Bailey Bedford OBs at the main terminus in Piccadilly, York. Both JXE60, at the back, and AEN63, at the front, are now cream. They are outside William Dove and Sons Ltd where the business had its 'works and foundry'. They were in business as 'Ironmongers, Iron & Steel Stockholders, Ironfounders, Heating and Domestic Engineers'. The window displays some of their dustbins, shovels and fencing products and their large shop in the town centre was on a continuation of Piccadilly, at 42 Parliament Street. They closed in June 1962 and the shop and foundry premises were put on the market. (Roy Marshall)

Bedford OB AEN63 is resting in Bolton, near Fangfoss, in July 1963. One of the drivers used to interrupt the ride from Pocklington for a spot of tea at his home in Bolton before carrying on to Fangfoss. The bus, barn and second house no longer exist. (Roy Marshall)

The Pocklington terminus was in Market Street by the Black Bull pub. However, OB GFU857 is clearly seen loading in Pocklington in October 1961 and is just south of Railway Street, suggesting the terminus was changed and was now opposite where EB started from. (PM Photography)

Market Street in Pocklington.

Leaving Stamford Bridge going towards York. (John Bennett)

Evidence of Bailey's excursion and private hire work is seen here with a Bailey's bus trip. The bus is HAL654 and was in the fleet from March 1949 to July 1956. (Andrew Sefton)

Bailey's 5025BT is on excursion/hire work in Scarborough. (John Bennett)

Hiring coaches to the West Yorkshire Road Car Company (WYRCC), especially in Leeds and Bradford, provided good income for many Yorkshire operators. DBT375C is in Keswick on hire to WYRCC for the X87 from Leeds and Bradford. (PM Photography)

The Post-War Fleet

As will be seen below, there were some livery variations. Initially, the livery was maroon with white/cream, but later this was reversed, probably in the mid 1950s, to reflect the increased use of coaches.

Bedford OB EWF644 was bought new in July 1947 and has the classic and common Duple Vista coach body. It is seen here on Piccadilly in York outside William Dove and Sons Ltd iron foundry and ironmongers. (Roy Marshall)

EWF664, seen here in the later livery, worked on until 1959. It is unknown what happened to it after that. (John Cockshott)

School's out with ACB123, a 1945 Bedford late OWB with a rare Duple Mark II bus body. In early 1947, Mulliner took over production of this body after Duple was overwhelmed with Vista coach bodying, and by this time had built around 250 Mark IIs on OWBs and OBs but mainly on the OBs. ACB123 came in March 1949 from Cronshaw in London NW4. It ran until March 1955 but has not been traced after that. (DS Giles)

HAL654 was a surprise 'heavyweight' purchase in 1949. This was a 1946 Leyland PS1 with a Duple body from Barton of Chilwell and shows the extra aluminium flashing that was common with Barton. This very bus was also modelled in Barton livery by Corgi in 1/43 scale. It is possible that Barton red and maroon livery was retained on what was a relatively new bus. Seen on 1 August 1955, when loading in Pocklington, it has York via Bishop Wilton on the blinds. It was withdrawn near its 10th birthday in July 1956 and worked then for the CEGB in Leeds on non-PSV work and was replaced at Bailey by a Commer RWF993. (John Cockshott)

After the Leyland PS1 from Barton came three Bedford OWBs with Roe, Mulliner and Duple bodies (HE9780/2 from Burrows of Wombwell and LML513) in February and March 1950. However, no pictures can be located. All were withdrawn by 1956.

EO6376 (below) was new in 1936 and was originally a Leyland TD4 from Barrow CT with an English Electric H56R body and was withdrawn in 1949. Bailey is also reported to have bought two single deckers from West Yorkshire. YG2193 was a 1933 Leyland TS4 and WX6688 was a 1933 Leyland TS1; both had 1936 ECOC C33F bodies.

The story goes that EO6376 had an ECOC body from WX6688 but that it never ran in service; the double decker may also have been used as a store and many former bus chassis became cattle wagons. However, it was photographed on 1 August 1955 by John Cockshott, the same day as HAL654 (above) and certainly looks to have not run for some time. Indeed, the offside front wheel looks strange. (John Cockshott)

COR880, new in 1948 to Streamways, Penarth, is another Bedford OB/Duple and was with BBS from June 1951 until May 1962 when it became a mobile shop. COR880 has an unusual black on white linen destination, maybe to match the painted name. Bailey was rather sloppy with destination screens and often seem not to have changed them. Indeed, COR880 is still going to York.

Before COR880 came JUB126, another Bedford OWB, in early 1951. It had a Duple body from Wallace Arnold and stayed until 1954, its tenth birthday. (Roy Marshall)

JXE60 was another delightful OB and was new in 1947. It was with BBS until 1963 when it then did further work with Hirst in Bradford as a non-PSV. It was replaced at Bailey by 8459WF, which was appropriately a Bedford VAS. JXE60 has a 'standard' Duple C29F body and was bought in February 1952 from Stronach in Selby. It shows a blank destination. (PM Photography)

FT6282 was another Bedford OB bought from Stronach in Selby in February 1952, this one being new in 1948. With BBS until January 1959, it also became a mobile shop. (Roy Marshall)

AEN63 came in April 1955, and earlier in June 1954 had come another OB, HXB724. This was from 1946 and was delivered to Orange in London SW2. It stayed with Bailey until January 1958. AEN63 was new in 1951 to Auty's Tours, Bury, and came from Allison, Eye, near Peterborough, and had replaced ACB123 at Bailey. It stayed until January 1966. (Roy Marshall)

The first new bus since 1947 was OWF363, and it entered service in April 1955. It was a Bedford SBG with a futuristic-looking Yeates Rivera C36F body. Its time with BBS was short and it was withdrawn in November 1957, going to Norths in Derby. (PM Photography)

Another Bedford OB came in July 1955, this one from Illingworth in Crigglestone, near Wakefield. CHL679 was new in 1950, served BBS until November 1967 and was another bus to be, appropriately, replaced by a Bedford VAS. (Roy Marshall)

In July 1956, another new bus was bought, this time a Commer Avenger III with a Plaxton C41F body, registered RWF993, which replaced Leyland HAL654. A picture has not been found of RWF993 but UUB403 (above), Wallace Arnold's special 7ft 6in version for Devon, was similarly bodied. RWF993 stayed until April 1964 and went to an operator in Kinver, Staffordshire. (John Cockshott)

GFU857 came from Lincolnshire RCC in March 1958 and was new in 1950. It replaced HXB924. It was Bailey's last OB to be withdrawn in October 1968 and is here at Piccadilly, York, with the intriguing destination 'York via Pocklington'. Perhaps some buses started, say, in Bishop Wilton and went via Pocklington to Fangfoss and Stamford Bridge for York? Timetables examined so far, however, suggest not. (Roy Marshall)

UWF193 was new in March 1958, ready for summer seasonal work. It had a Yeates Europa body on a Commer Avenger chassis; this high chassis is distinguished on these bodies by the extra corner windows below the windscreen to facilitate vision of kerbs. It is seen here in Leeds in the Wellington Street bus overflow area used on summer Saturdays. It was on hire to West Yorkshire RCC for a trip to Bridlington. Other pictures show the same bus without the lower red livery. Withdrawn in June 1965, it went to Hutchinson of Husthwaite, to the north of York. (John Bennett)

MDN385 was one of four Bedford SBGs acquired by Bailey from Tanton of York in January 1959. Two had Burlingham bodies and two had Duple bodies. The coaches were new between 1953 and 1956 and three left Bailey within a few months, the other in October 1960. All were sold on to other operators and Burlingham-bodied HRN416 went to Hope of Terrington. MDN385, shown below with a Duple Vega body, initially went to an operator in Armadale in West Lothian but is seen here on 3 August 1963 opposite Wellington Street bus station with Knowles of Oulton, near Leeds, and is on hire to West Yorkshire RCC. (John Cockshott)

1946BT was a new bus to Bailey in April 1960 and had been preceded by YDH573, a 1957 Commer Avenger IV with a Duple body that had been purchase from Central in Walsall in March 1959. It left in October 1960 after it had two summer seasons and went to an operator in Norfolk.

1946BT was also a Commer Avenger IV but with a flamboyant Yeates body. It has a 'Europa' body badging. However, it looks remarkably similar to the later Yeates Fiesta body style and was possibly a prototype. 1946BT stayed with Bailey until August 1973 and, as shown above, did stage bus work and is outside the square box building that replaced the William Dove factory. (Peter Henson)

February 1961 brought 5025BT, another Commer with a Yeates body; this one had the Fiesta body (and badging). It went in February 1972 and was replaced by a Bedford VAM VBF404D. (Donald Hudson)

VWR586 was the first modern small bus for Bailey and came in April 1962, replacing Bedford OB GOR880. New in 1958 to Drake of Scholes in West Yorkshire, it was a Bedford C5Z1 with a Duple C29F body. Withdrawn in October 1966, it stayed local with Gray's of Stamford Bridge. (PM Photography)

8459WF is seen here near to York FC ground. Bought new in June 1963, it was a Bedford VAS1 with a Plaxton body and had replaced Bedford OB JXE60. It stayed until June 1976 when it went to Johnson of Brandesburton, a small village seven miles west of Hornsea. Probably as a result of the change in ownership from 1961, the Bailey's fleet name design was changed and 8459WF shows an early version. (John Bennett)

Showing the next style of fleet name is 574BWF, a Bedford VA14 with a Plaxton body, which was new April 1964. It looks to be away from its home area, possibly in the Yorkshire Dales. (PM Photography)

574BWF is back home having just run over the River Ouse onto Station Road whilst passing through York on school work. Frankish of Brandesburton was the owner after August 1973. (PM Photography)

DBT375C is at Piccadilly, York, on stage work with no destination indicators, most probably because of laziness or complacency. A Bedford SB13 with a Duple Bella Vega body, it was new in June 1965. It worked regularly on the stage routes until early 1983 and was then scrapped. (John Bennett)

New in 1954 to Davies of Leigh, STJ787 was likely bought in December 1965 for the stage routes. This Bedford SBO with a Duple Vega body has the oval grill that came after Bedford's own panel and before the 'butterfly' grill design (as seen on VWR586 on page 51). The destination blind in the nearside upper front glazing may be noted along with some newspapers to be dropped off. (John Bennett)

The offside of STJ787, complete with driver in braces and mid-body, deep gouge damage. Behind is West Riding AEC Reliance with a Roe B41D body from 1961; West Riding ran in from Selby to York. On the left is a York Pullman AEC Regal from 1951 but with a Roe body from 1963.

March 1967 brought HWF420E, a new Bedford VAL14 with a Duple Vega Major C52F body. It would be five years before any other bus entered service. This was an unusual and rare use on the stage service but clearly has the blinds (even though it is going to York via Stamford Bridge). It had left Bailey by June 1984 and became a stock car transporter. (John Bennett)

In April 1967 came JWF113E, a Bedford VAS5 with a Duple Vista 25 C29F body. It had left Bailey by June 1984 and became a caravan. (PM Photography)

In April 1972 came VBF404D from Daniel of York, which was new to Harper Bros of Heath Hayes in 1966. Another Bedford, this time a VAM14 with a Duple Viscount C45F body, it largely took over the stage work from STJ787. Bailey looks to have totally given up on destination blinds and also are back to a plain style of fleet name. (Roy Marshall)

VBF404D is getting ready to depart. In December 1978, this bus was reported as withdrawn but was still in the depot in September 1981. However, it had gone by July 1982. (Peter Henson)

The other main service bus in the early 1970s was HBT753L, a Bedford YRT bought new in August 1973 with a Plaxton Panorama Express body. Here it has a correct destination blind. HBT753L worked until the end of May 1983 and then went over to Ingleby. (Peter Henson)

GBT138D was new in April 1966 to Milburn, t/a Leavening Motor Services, and was bought by Bailey in April 1975. This Bedford SB5 had a Plaxton Embassy IV C41F body and was withdrawn and stored by March 1983 before going to a Barnsley dealer in February 1984. (PM Photography)

OVY203T, here loading on Piccadilly in the rain, was Bailey's last new purchase in December 1978 and was a Ford R1114 with a Plaxton Supreme Express C53F body. It also worked until May 1985 and then went to Ingleby. (Roy Marshall)

Bailey's next to last bus was RWY701M, a Bedford YRT that was new in March 1974 to Furness of High Green and bought by Bailey in June 1982 from Taylor of Dinnington. It had a Plaxton body and also passed over to Ingleby in May 1985. The last bus bought by Bailey came in July 1983 from Skills in Nottingham. It was FAU46L, a Leyland PSU5/4R with a Plaxton C53F body. Below is its sister, FAU45L, with Skills. FAU46L ran with Bailey in Skills' livery for over two years and only received Bailey's livery after the takeover. (Mineralcraft)

After Bailey were owned by Ingleby, the first bus bought was PTT106R, a Bristol LH6L (only 7ft 6ins wide) with a Plaxton Supreme Express C45F body. New in February 1977 to Western National, it was withdrawn from the associated North Devon company in March 1985 and came to Ingleby; it entered service in Western National green livery. The blue front wheel indicates what was soon to come. (Peter Henson)

PTT106R in Ingleby's blue livery, complete with side lettering showing 'Daily Service–York–Stamford Bridge–Pocklington'. Still keeping Bailey's name, it is at the new loading point of York railway station. In January 1988, PTT109R moved on and went to three different operators. In April 1998, it was sold for preservation. This failed and it was scrapped in 2010. (Peter Henson)

Chapter 3

J. Broadbent, Stamford Bridge

History and Development

John Broadbent was born in 1899 and went on to serve in the Royal Navy during the First World War. His early life is not known but his parents came from Liverpool. In 1927, John married a local girl in Stamford Bridge and started a bus company from his home in Frances Street, York, along with a garage at Oxtoby's yard on Piccadilly in York.

From there he initially operated a few small Morris Model T buses, which were used on private hire and excursion work and numbered from 1 upwards. The number series ran to 41 in 1982, although six buses were not numbered (seven in some listings) and it also seems that number 28 was not used.

Meanwhile, in 1929, land was bought in Stamford Bridge, five miles east of York. This was developed into Danes Well Garage, the home for the business; the stage route, described later, had also been started.

Two of Broadbent's first buses were captured on film around 1934 when they were involved in a large annual children's excursion to Filey, which was organised by the York Poor Children's Fresh Air Fund.

The second bus bought by Broadbent was WF2143. All that is known about it is that it had a Morris T chassis and the body had 14 seats.

WF3075 was Broadbent's fourth bus and was a Chevrolet with a Barnaby body for 14 passengers. It was new in February 1930.

The excursion was an exceptionally large organised event and, for example, in 1939, 1,600 children went on the trip. It was reported then, 'it is some 30 years since Sir William Forster Todd initiated this annual event'. Therefore, in the early years rail would have been used. Funds were raised from donations and attendance at 'entertainments'. In 1939, for example, the buses left York for Filey, where a meal was taken in the school room, following which, 'sports were organised by the Committee on the sands; and also, in that year 'each child will receive sixpence to spend… given by Mr George Turner of the Empire in York'.

It took quite some organisation, requiring many buses and a lot of supervision. Also, in 1939, it ran on a Thursday, the York market day when extra stage bus services were already required. Therefore, this excursion would have had to draw in buses from all over the county and buses from Everingham, West Yorkshire Road Car and Corcoran of Tadcaster were amongst those know to have been used.

The Stage Route

York, like other places in the late 1920s, was experiencing a steady growth of stage bus services and already operating in the eastern area of York were the independents Everingham, Bailey and York Pullman.

John Broadbent maybe thought he also would have a go, and he started a service from York, Piccadilly, to Full Sutton. This ran via Gate Helmsley, Stamford Bridge, Low Catton, High Catton and the Full Sutton Brickyards. The initial hearing over the route was in December 1931 under the 1930 Road Traffic Act that had come into force in April. Broadbent must have been operating prior to February 1931, otherwise his application would not have been considered, and they must have used a pub or private land in York as no York Hackney licence records exist for Broadbent.

At the December 1931 hearing, it had been noted by an opposer that there were 39 buses operating between York and Stamford Bridge at intervals of 15 minutes. Mr Broadbent agreed that only 286 people lived in High and Low Catton with fewer in Full Sutton and 490 in Stamford Bridge. However, he thought there was room for him on Saturdays, Mondays and Thursdays. The opponents, however,

6700WF runs over the bridge in Stamford Bridge. (John Bennett)

submitted that the route was already well covered and the complaint was initially upheld. However, Broadbent appealed and an inquiry was held. At the inquiry, Broadbent eventually withdrew the request for Mondays and Thursdays and asked for Saturdays on the basis of his current timetable. An agreement was reached between the parties in May 1932 and the inquiry was closed.

It has also been recorded that the route only ran on Sundays, but specific evidence of this has not been found. Meanwhile, the 1948 and 1955 timings were as follows:

J. BROADBENT. 'Fairfield', STAMFORD BRIDGE, Yorks. (1955) T

SATURDAY SERVICE ONLY.

		a.m.	p.m.	p.m.	p.m.
FULL SUTTON	Dep.		12.40.		5.40.
BRICKYARDS	"	8.45.	12.44.		5.44.
HIGH CATTON	"	8.49.	12.48.		5.48.
LOW CATTON	"	9.00.	12.52.		5.52.
STAMFORD BRIDGE	"	9.05.	1.00.	1.00.	6.00.
GATE HELMSLEY	"	9.09.	1.04.	1.04.	6.04.
YORK	Arr.	9.30.	1.24.	1.24.	6.24.

YORK	Dep.	11.30.	4.15.		9.30.
GATE HELMSLEY	"	11.50.	4.35.		9.50.
STAMFORD BRIDGE	"	11.54.	4.39.		9.54.
LOW CATTON	"	11.58.	4.43.		9.58.
HIGH CATTON	"	12.02.	4.47.		10.02.
BRICKYARDS	"	12.06.	4.51.		10.06.
FULL SUTTON	Arr.		4.55.		10.10.

'Fairfield' was the family home of Mr Broadbent's wife. Why the 1p.m. from Stamford Bridge is shown twice is not known!

As already noted, other independent companies also ran between York and Stamford Bridge, and a comparison of the timings shows that in the early 1950s there were 27 departures on a Saturday.

Ex-York	Operator	Ex-York	Operator
0655	York Pullman	1600	York Pullman
0745	York Pullman	1630	Bailey
0830	Bailey	1700	York Pullman
0900	York Pullman	1730	Everingham
1000	York Pullman	1800	York Pullman
1030	Everingham	1830	Everingham
1100	York Pullman	1900	York Pullman
1130	Broadbent and Bailey	2030	Bailey
1230	Bailey	2100	York Pullman
1300	York Pullman	2130	Broadbent and Everingham
1400	York Pullman	2200	York Pullman
1430	Everingham	2300	Bailey
1500	York Pullman		

Journey Times: Bailey, 30 mins; Broadbent, 24 mins; Everingham, 25 mins; York Pullman, 25 mins.

This comparison shows many 'every 30 minutes' coordinated timings. However, the two of Broadbent's departures at the same times as others may reflect peak requirements.

The Company Grows

After the earlier new, late-1920s Morris and Chevrolet small buses, from 1936 Broadbent replaced the fleet with the ubiquitous Bedford WTB model; one had a Barnaby of Hull body and the others were by Plaxton of Scarborough. At least two of the Plaxtons stayed in the fleet until 1953, an image of one being used on the company letterhead in 1948 is shown below.

COACHES for HIRE

Tel. Stamford Bridge 228

J. BROADBENT   DANES WELL GARAGE, STAMFORD BRIDGE, YORK

By 1939, Broadbent had at least three of the WTBs operating, and from 1940 some of them will have worked on contract services that started for Derwent Plastics Ltd of Stamford Bridge. This company had been established in 1934, when a former brewery was converted into a workshop and then into a factory.

The Second World War brought expansion to Broadbent and between 1943 and 1945, four Bedford OWBs came. This was because of military work; an ammunition factory was built in Stamford Bridge and an airfield was being constructed at Full Sutton. The airfield opened in 1944, under the RAF Bomber command operating the Handley Page Halifax. The airfield remained under military ownership until April 1963 and since then has been used as a civilian airfield.

Post-war, Derwent Plastics expanded, and Broadbent became more heavily involved in providing contract transport work, bringing workers to the factory from the surrounding rural area. A work pattern now developed for Broadbent with Derwent contract work and school contracts on Mondays to Fridays, and then on the weekends, excursion work and in the summer, the hire of coaches to operators like West Yorkshire Road Car. Also, on Saturdays the stage service tied up one bus.

An Broadbent excursion with 32-6700WF accompanied by UAS REs and two Plaxton coaches. (John Bennett)

Broadbent is on hire to West Yorkshire in the 1970s, and 36-RBT654G is in Lancaster on the Leeds/Bradford express X88 route to Morecambe.

38-GWF983L on a contract run into York.

The Derwent Plastics factory site was enlarged in the 1950s and 1960s and new buildings were erected. The contract services for Derwent Plastics expanded and grew to include the following destinations:

- York.
- Malton via Buttercrambe, Gally Gap and Westow.
- Pocklington via Bugthorpe, Garrowby, Bishop Wilton and Meltonby.
- Pocklington via Full Sutton, Fangfoss, Bolton and Yapham Mill.
- Pocklington via Full Sutton, Fangfoss, Bolton and Yapham Mill; returning via Barmby Moor and Wilberfoss to Stamford Bridge.

It will be seen that these contract routes largely ran along the same routes as Everingham's and Bailey's stage buses.

In August 1957, John Broadbent died and to ensure continuance of work bus operations, Derwent Plastics bought the business and, therefore, on 23 August 1957, J. Broadbent Motors Limited was formed. The following extract from *Commercial Motor*, dated 30 August 1957, gives further details, including an objection from Bailey's Bus Service of Fangfoss:

Customers Buy Operator's Business

The Yorkshire Traffic Commissioners last week granted an application by J. Broadbent (Motors), Ltd., York, to operate work people's services from Stamford Bridge to York, Pocklington and Malton for Derwent Plastics, Ltd., Stamford Bridge, who acquired Broadbent's last month.

The services had been run since 1940 by Mr J. Broadbent and the application was consequent upon the incorporation of the applicant concern.

Mr J. Bailey, Stamford Bridge, objected to the applicants serving Pocklington. He said that he was losing money in maintaining his services.

Mr L. R. Cornelius, a director of the Derwent and Broadbent companies, said that until the acquisition of the applicants, Derwent had arranged with 'Mr. Broadbent to carry their workpeople and no deductions had been made from the wages of persons carried. It had now been decided, however, to deduct contributions because Derwent were faced with rising costs'.

In January 1960, the stage service finished, leaving Broadbent with the contract work along with excursions and private hires. However, Derwent Plastics were growing, and their products for the automotive industry, made using injection moulding manufacturing to make plastic components, were supplied to a fast-developing automotive industry. As Derwent Plastics grew, so did Broadbent, and in 1961 Danes Well Garage was expanded.

The York terminus of the stage route on Piccadilly was near to its junction with Coppergate. Over the wall is the Merchants Coffee House and, joining that, the Merchant Adventurers Hall in Fossgate. Here is 2882BT parked by the original bus stop in Piccadilly, some 10 years after the route stopped. The loading point was near to the town centre, whereas Bailey and Everingham stopped 200 yards further down Piccadilly, behind the photographer. (John Bennett)

The 1970s were a relatively stable times for Broadbent, apart from normal fleet purchases/disposals. Derwent Plastics became a subsidiary of McKechnie Plastic Components, with factories in Stamford Bridge and Pickering, and employed 420 people.

However, the 1980s became a game changer for Broadbent. First, in May 1980, the licences for some of the contract routes were not renewed. These were the Malton and the two Pocklington via Full Sutton routes, which left the York and the Pocklington via Bishop Wilton routes with Broadbent.

Next, in 1982, Derwent Plastics decided to sell Broadbent. In January 1983, Reynard bought J. Broadbent Motors Limited along with eight buses and the York and the Pocklington via Bishop Wilton contract routes. Five of Broadbent's buses soon left and five second-hand Fords with Plaxton bodies were purchased as replacements, which then ran with the three retained Broadbent buses.

Broadbent Fleet from the 1940s

The fleet size, as already has been mentioned was, from the late 1920s to the late 1930s, between two and four buses. Wartime growth and the start of the Derwent Plastics contract work pushed the fleet to its largest size of 12 or 13 buses. After the war, the 1950s and 1960s fleets were consistently at nine or ten buses. However, from 1967 to 1972, this fell to six or seven buses. After 1972, the fleet grew to eight buses and this was largely maintained until the sale in 1983.

After the four Bedford OWBs bought during the Second World War, Broadbent bought another one, new in 1943 to Simpson of Ripon, which came to Broadbent in 1948. 14-EWF487 is waiting on Piccadilly, York, between journeys. It stayed with Broadbent until 1954, when it became a mobile shop in Crigglestone, near Wakefield.

The next purchase in the 1940s was a new Bedford OB with a Duple body (16-DVY948) followed by 17-HBT561, a Dennis Lancet 3 with a Yeates coach body. These purchases were then duplicated in 1950 and 1951 with an OB (18-HWF557) and another Dennis (21-KBT218 – see right) with a Yeates body. The Dennis stayed from August 1951 to May 1960 and then went to work with other small operators until 1965. However, the new OB (HWF557) stayed for some time and outlasted the subsequent second-hand OBs before being withdrawn in February 1967.

19-JU3838 is seen with its March 1934 original owner, Brown Bros of Sapcote, Leicester, who withdrew it in March 1950. Two months later, JU3838 was sold to Bermuda Motor Services in Nuneaton. Not long after, it came to Broadbent in July 1950 and stayed until September 1951. (The Bus Archive)

20-KHY327 came to Broadbent in May 1951 from Eagle Coaches, Bristol, and left Broadbent in January 1953. It is seen here with Hylton & Dawson of Glenfield, Leicestershire, who bought it in June 1953. It stayed with them until December 1960 when it was sold for scrap. (Peter Yeomans)

In 1953 and 1954 came four second-hand OBs, all with 'standard' Duple Vista bodies (22 to 25, LTD62, KOJ484, DRP900, HWU593). Representative of the Bedford OB purchases is 24-DRP900, new in 1947, and, from 1950, 23-KOJ484. DRP900 came from York Brothers in Northampton where it was named *HMS London* and KOJ484 came from Sandwell Motors in Birmingham. Shown parked up in Piccadilly, York, with steamy windows and radiator covers, DRP900 was withdrawn in 1958 and went to a contractor in Coventry, whereas KOJ484 stayed until 1963 before going to the dealer, Yeates, in Loughborough. Broadbent bought four new Yeates bodies between 1949 and 1960. (Roy Marshall)

From 1955 to 1972 Bedford were the chassis of choice with a range of coach bodies. The first, acquired in April 1955, was a 1951 Bedford SB, 26-CCP148, with a 1951 Duple body and was new to Holdsworth of Halifax. No other buses came after 26 until the 1958 new purchase (27-UWF600) of a Bedford SB3 with a Duple Vega body.

29-WBT909 was a Bedford SB3 with a Yeates body, new in January 1959, and is seen here on school duties being pursued by 31-2882BT, a similar coach from 1960. (John Bennett)

A surprise buy, perhaps, in 1960 was 30-ERU603. It was a 1939 Bristol K5G from Hants & Dorset that had been rebodied in 1954 with a body from another ERU-registered vehicle. Shown here at the depot as Broadbent fleet number 30 (it has also been reported to have not been numbered), ERU603 stayed until 1966 and was re-engined in 1962 with an AEC engine. Alongside it is 2882BT, fleet number 31 (and not 30 as has also been recorded). (John Sinclair)

Fleet number 31 (shown just below the first side window) is on excursion work in the Yorkshire Dales. 2882BT is a Bedford SB1 with a Yeates body that was new in May 1960 and stayed until 1975. (R. F. Mack)

32-6700WF was a Bedford SB5 with a Duple Bella Vega body. Seen in June 1974, it was new in February 1963, withdrawn in March 1978 and then scrapped. The reflective number plate seems inappropriate. (John Bennett)

From the mid-1960s, Broadbent bought standard buses, mainly Bedfords with Plaxton bodies. Space limitations for this book mean these cannot be shown. The contract fleet also received a Bristol FLF from Bristol OC and a Leyland single decker from Ribble. Then, as mentioned earlier, in January 1983, Reynard bought Broadbent, something that also was to happen to the next operator, Milburn.

Chapter 4

Milburn of Leavening

(trading as Leavening Motor Services)

A Milburn Bedford OB waits at Leavening Crossroads to leave for Malton. The Jolly Farmer pub can be seen in the background. (Roy Marshall)

Introduction

Leavening is one of the southernmost villages in the district of Ryedale and lies in North Yorkshire. It is on the northern foothills of a region of chalky rolling hills called the Yorkshire Wolds, six miles south of Malton and some 15 miles northeast of York. There are many small villages tucked away in the valleys and on hills, often with a pub and a post office/general store to serve a small population. Travel to the nearest market town for shopping and entertainment was common, with Malton on a Friday and Saturday or York on a Thursday and Saturday.

History

The company origins go back to a carting service run by horse and cart to York by Ernest Milburn. He was the son of John Milburn, born in 1866, who was a corn miller and farmer. In 1927, at the age of 30, Ernest started operating a bus service into Malton on Tuesdays, Fridays and Saturdays.

Little has been recorded about the subsequent years, but it is known that some route development took place as the following timeline shows:

- A route on Saturday from Leavening to Scarborough was stopped in 1951.
- A route from Leavening to Malton via Leppington started in the mid 1950s.
- In 1957, a route from Thixendale to Malton started and probably operated as a 3-mile extension from Leavening.

In 1957, Ernest died, so two of his sons, Alan and Maurice, took over the company. Years later, the following developments took place:

- The route to York finished in May 1967.
- The route to Thixendale stopped in October 1968.
- In August 1969, the daily service from Leavening to Malton was stopped on Mondays, Wednesdays and Thursdays and only ran on Tuesdays, Fridays and Saturdays with a reduced number of journeys. In the *Yorkshire Post* on 6 August 1969, Maurice Milburn said: 'We are losing money, nearly everybody runs their own car these days. It has been building up over the past two or three years, but it is a common thing in rural areas.'

In 1969, the fleet was also reduced from five to four buses when an OB and an SB were replaced by just one SB. This change, however, made no difference to the existing school work undertaken as both the Milburns drove, along with a part-time driver.

In April 1976, the Saturday extension to Malton from Acklam via Leavening, which was just under a mile in length, was discontinued. In December 1981, one of the sons, S. P. Milburn, entered the business, and in January 1987, Milburn sold out to Reynard-Pullman who took the five buses in the fleet at that time. The routes were abandoned by Reynard-Pullman and partly passed over to West Yorkshire Road Car who ran them from their Malton depot. Reynard-Pullman used the garage as an outstation and the building remained the property of the Milburn brothers.

In February 1990, 20 of the Reynard-Pullman coach fleet, along with the York Pullman trading name, were sold to Hull City Transport who, as York Pullman Coaches Limited, continued for a few years trading from the former Milburn and Broadbent Stamford Bridge premises.

Routes

From	To	Via	Days of operating	Max. journeys and journey time	Started/ finished
Leavening (Crossroads)*	Malton (Market Place)	Burythorpe, Kennythorpe, Langton, Birdsall	Monday to Friday	4	By 1932 / finished in Jan 1987 and became part of WYRCC route 83/85
			Tuesday and Friday	+ 3 =Σ 7	
			Saturday*	7 see below*	
				Full route 45 mins	
Leavening (Crossroads)**	York (St Denys Road)	Howsham, Harton	Saturday	1 45 mins	By 1932 / May 1967
Acklam	Malton	Leavening, Burythorpe, Kennythorpe, then direct	Saturday	2 35 mins	By 1932 / Apr 1976
Leavening	Scarborough	Norton, Rillington, Low Moor, Heslerton, Ganton	Thursday	1 90 mins	By 1932 / gone by 1951
Thixendale	Malton	Via Leavening and the normal route?	Saturday	?	August 1957 / October 1968
Leavening***	Malton	Leppington, Howsham, Westow, Firby, Mennethorpe	Friday	?	Started between 1954 and 1979 / finished in January 1987 and became WYRCC route 85A

  * The Saturday service to Malton used two buses and, at least from 1939 to 1965, there were seven journeys ex-Leavening. Most went direct to Malton, omitting the weekday journeys via Langton and/or Birdsall; these direct journeys took 30 minutes. In 1951, two of these journeys also started from Acklam and had a 10-minute journey to Leavening. Langton and Birdsall were served on a Saturday by intermediate services from Malton to Birdsall (three journeys to Malton, taking 15 minutes) and to Langton (three journeys to Malton, taking 25 mins); these Saturday Birdsall and Langton timings were operationally covered by running round trips from Malton. The 1937 timetable also has a similar pattern including the two buses on the last departure ex-Malton leaving at the same time, with bus one going to Birdsall, then straight to Leavening on a road not normally used, whereas, bus two ran to Langton, then on the normal route via Kennythorpe, etc.

  ** Bailey of Fangfoss had a service from Bugthorpe to York on Thursdays and Saturdays, which was withdrawn in September 1960. Milburn's existing Saturday service duplicated the route from Gally Gap, Horsham and Horton into York.

  *** Bailey's relatively frequent service to Malton via Stamford Bridge was withdrawn north of Stamford Bridge in September 1955. It is possible that this Milburn route, which is known to have started after 1954, could have offered some replacement on a Friday as the service largely duplicates the former Bailey route from Leppington and Westow into Malton.

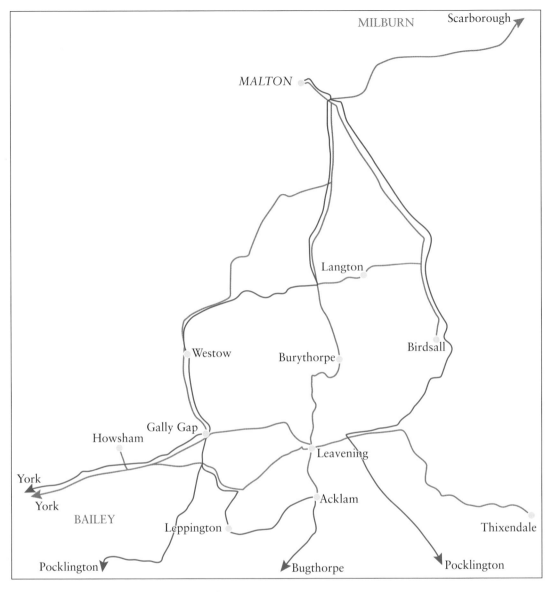

All Milburn's services used the Market Place terminus in Malton; this was not enclosed as some images may suggest, but opened straight onto the road, with buses reversing in to park. Here, 7893BT looks to have a carton waiting to be loaded and is alongside a similar Bedford from Ryedale Motors. A double decker (MUM275) from Hardwicks is at the end. (Roy Marshall)

As already partly mentioned, Bailey of Fangfoss had three routes that came near to Milburn's sphere of operation. Bailey had at one time two routes from Pocklington to Malton:

- One passed just under half a mile to the east of Leavening for Birdsall and Malton. This very rural route lasted until June 1951 and had run three Saturday-only trips.
- The other route came via Stamford Bridge and ran to the west of Leavening near to Leppington for Westow and Malton. This ran seven days a week with seven trips on a Saturday and was withdrawn, north of Stamford Bridge, in September 1955.
- The third Bailey route came from Bugthorpe, near Stamford Bridge, to York. It passed though nearby Acklam and Leppington and then went west to parallel Milburn's route via Howsham and Harton for York. Bailey had just the one journey on Thursdays and Saturdays and their route finished in September 1960.

Fleet

The early fleet is not fully recorded, but from 1939 two Bedford WTBs, probably with Plaxton bodies, came, followed in April 1947 by a new OB, then in December a 1933 Bedford WLB came from Hugill in Malton and ran for just two years.

From 1948, the fleet is well recorded and is illustrated below. The fleet strength from 1947 to 1987 was four or five buses at any one time and the majority of the buses were bought new, 90 per cent being Bedfords.

The livery was medium green and cream, apart from one bus that was blue.

FWF489 is a Bedford OB (and not a WLB as in some listings) and was new in May 1948 with a Plaxton body. During a busy Saturday at Malton it is parked alongside Milburn's JOF332, which has the more usual Duple Vista body. Probably, this was before 1715 hours when there were departures to Leavening direct and one to Langton via Birdsall. FWF489 was withdrawn in September 1959 and was replaced by a rebodied Bedford OWB, KRE539.

The East Yorkshire 1956 Regent V shows its Beverley Bar roof-shaped body and has a youth leaning out of a top window. It worked East Yorkshire's route from Driffield which had three alternative routes: the direct 34A via Burdale and Wetwang with, in 1966, two journeys on a Saturday taking 55 mins; the indirect 34B via Burdale and Fridaythorpe with one Saturday journey taking 70 mins; and the even more indirect 34 via Weaverthorpe and Sledmere that took 89 mins and had ten journeys spread over the week but none on a Monday or Wednesday! (Roy Marshall)

A 1950 Plaxton-bodied OB, HBT880, by the Employment Office on St Denys Road in York on the one 45-minute Saturday journey. Pre-war, it left Leavening at 0730 hours and departed York at 1130 hours. By 1951, it left an hour later but still left York at 1130 hours. Once back at Leavening, it was available to work as the second bus on the Malton route. The pre-war terminus in York was outside Reynard's Garage on Piccadilly, but this was changed, sometime between 1951 and 1954, to the nearby St Denys Road. Piccadilly is just down the hill past the Employment Office and Reynard's Garage was to the right, next to the Employment Office.

The route was closed in May 1967 but HBT880 had been withdrawn in April 1966 and was replaced by Bedford SB5 GBT138D. (Roy Marshall)

Malton in May 1959 with RBT16, new in December 1955, that had replaced a 1947 Bedford, registered EWF702. RBT16 is a Bedford SBG with a Plaxton Venturer III C37F body and had a relatively short stay with Milburn as it was withdrawn in June 1961 and was replaced by Bedford SB3/Plaxton 7893BT. RBT16 passed through five operators until being finally withdrawn in 1970. Alongside it is a Bedford OB from Robinson of Pickering who traded as Ryedale Motors and ran many routes two/three times a week, with some just once a week. These were from Malton (three routes) and from Pickering (four routes). Some routes were withdrawn in 1965 and all had closed by 1968. (John Cockshott)

JOF332 is in Malton with Milburn FWF489 and East Yorkshire VKH42. New in 1948 to Smith Imperial Coaches, Birmingham, it came via two other operators and entered service with Milburn in November 1957, replacing a 1939 Bedford WTB. With a Duple Vista body, it has the rarer Vista V Service Coach body, which was built to conserve materials, and is, therefore, without the waistband flaring and a sliding roof; the Vista V was built for only four months from late 1948. JOF332 was withdrawn after five years with Milburn and went to the dealer, Moseley, in Loughborough. It was replaced by an interesting second-hand Bedford J4LZ2, registered NJR544. (Roy Marshall)

KRE539 was a 1942 Bedford OWB, with a Roe utility bus body, that was new to Worthington of Stafford. It was with two other operators before coming to Milburn in October 1959 as a replacement for FWF489 and had been rebodied in May 1950 with this Duple Vista C29F body. Alongside it is a Wallace Arnold-livered AEC Reliance/Plaxton Panorama I with subsidiary Hardwick's Services. KRE539 was withdrawn in April 1969 when it went to Stillington Traction Engine Committee and was replaced at Milburn by Bedford SB5 RWF83G. (PM Photography)

Wallace Arnold AEC Reliance/Plaxton Panorama Is had been used by WAT subsidiary Hardwicks Services of Snainton (the subject of another book by the author). They were from the series 9203 to 9206NW and used by Hardwicks from 1965 until 1967 (9206), in 1968 (9203) and in 1969 (9204/5). Hardwicks had a two-journey Saturday-only PAYE route to Malton from Ebberston and Scarborough. This took 85 mins and the arriving bus would lay over in Malton for 90 minutes before returning. Just visible alongside is Milburn OB KRE539 (see page 75).

Again at Malton, 7893BT is a 1961 Bedford SB3 with a Plaxton Embassy C41F body and replaced RBT16. Withdrawn in in May 1972, it went to Castle Coaches in Bolsover. (Roy Marshall)

An unusual bus, NJR544 was new in November 1958 to Armstrong of Westerhope and came to Milburn in April 1962 to replace OB JOF332. Here in Malton on 13 July 1966, it is a Bedford J4LZ2 with a Plaxton C29F body and was a directly sized replacement for the OBs. It stayed for five years before being replaced by 949AWW. (John Cockshott)

GBT138D was another Bedford SB5 but with a Plaxton Embassy IV body and is shown here at York Football Club. New in April 1966 to replace the long-serving OB HBT880, it was withdrawn in 1975. It then passed to Baileys Bus Service of Fangfoss; it is illustrated on page 55. (John Bennett)

949AWW was new to Rossie Motors in Rossington in 1962. It is seen with Rossie on 23 June 1962 at Glasgow Paddocks in Doncaster. It was a Bedford SB5 with a Duple Northern Gannet body, which was effectively the former Burlingham Seagull 62 body with a restyled front. It came to Milburn in April 1967 to replace NJR544 and went relatively soon, in May 1968, being replaced by EYG551C. (John Cockshott)

Not illustrated is another second-hand buy in May 1968, EYG551C, which was new in 1965 to Howard of Brinsworth and quickly bought, it seems, to replace 949AWW. It was the last second-hand purchase and was another Bedford SB5 with the front-side silver-sided Plaxton Panorama body (otherwise it was like the Embassy IV). EYG551C stayed five years and then went, via Hughes dealers in Cleckheaton, to Heald Coaches of Waterfoot.

Shown is another Bedford SB5, new in June 1969, with a Plaxton Panorama II body. RWF83G had replaced the last Bedford OB, KRE539, and stayed until August 1978. RWF83G then saw service with two other operators.

In May 1972, CBT269K brought Milburn into the underfloor engines era with this Bedford YRQ, which replaced the Bedford VAM and has a Plaxton Elite Express body. Designed for PAYE operations, it is seen here outside the Black Swan in Malton Market Place on a wet day and looks to have rolls of newspapers on the dashboard. Whilst the Black Swan building is still there, it is no longer a pub. CBT269K had replaced Bedford SB3 7893BT and was sold in August 1980 to Alexcars in Cirencester who kept it for nine years. (Roy Marshall)

In April 1973 came GWF313L, one more Bedford SB5, this time with a Plaxton Panorama IV body. It replaced EYG551C, and quite why it was blue is a mystery. Perhaps it was in stock and was needed quickly and/or was a diverted order? It is seen here on a private hire by the Vice-Principal's house at St John's College, York, which in 2006 became a university. It was also sold, like CBT269K, in August 1980 and passed through three local operators before turning up with a football club in Shepshed, Leicestershire, in March 1988. (John Bennett)

GWF313L looks to be blue still as it stands alongside JVY754N, which was bought in March 1975. Another Bedford YRQ with a Plaxton Elite III body, it replaced GBT138D and then left Milburn by March 1982 for a local operator, Morse in Stillington. (PM Photography)

Before buying the above Ford in 1979, Milburn had two Bedford YLQs (like the YRQ but with a larger engine), both with Plaxton Supreme bodies, and these were new in 1976 and 1978. They were VDN773R and MBT244T and both had gone to other operators by 1986.

Ford VBT201V (above) was a change from the Bedfords and another Ford came in 1980, registered FDN244W. Whilst FDN was there at the end and went over to Reynard-Pullman in January 1987 (who had a large Ford fleet), VBT had left Milburn by July 1983 and did four years with Millman and Sons in Buckfastleigh. It is seen with Millman and looks to be still in Milburn's livery. (John Law)

EKH475Y was new in August 1982 and was a return to the Bedford/Plaxton Supreme; it was the YMP model that had succeeded the YLQ. It went over to the new owners, Reynard-Pullman, in January 1987.

The next three coaches, bought in 1983, 1984 and 1986, also passed to Reynard-Pullman and were all Plaxton Paramounts. Registered JBT421Y, B633LJU and C738TJF, all these were new, and whilst JBT421Y and C738TJF had the Bedford 11-metre YNT chassis, B633LJU was another change as it had a Leyland Tiger chassis.

Bedford JBT421Y, seen in Reynard-Pullman livery between January 1987 and February 1990, was one of 20 coaches sold to Hull City Transport with the York Pullman name in February 1990.

Bedford C738TJF in York Pullman Coach Company Limited livery after February 1990.

The New Era for Buses

Whilst the subsequent developments of the former stage bus routes of Milburn are beyond the scope of this book, it is interesting to highlight some of these. Deregulation and regular tendering for routes brought regular changes to the traditional country bus with, for example, new headways that were often worked by changed operators. This new norm can be rather confusing, but I will try to keep it simple!

Initially, after the sale of Milburn, West Yorkshire route 83 from Malton to York, which was operated from their depot in Malton, was diverted via Harton. Also, a new route 85 ran between Malton and Leavening via Burythorpe on Tuesdays, Fridays and Saturdays; there was an 85A on Fridays that went via Westow. These routes were changed in August 1987 with the 85 becoming route 83 from Malton to York but now via Leavening and Harton and the Friday 85A becoming the 85 from Malton to Leavening via Westow.

Subsequently, West Yorkshire Malton became Yorkshire Coastliner and following a re-tendering, Appleby took over in January 1996, then it was Vokes/Lawns of Market Weighton in 2000 and next was Hutchinson of Easingwold in December 2003. The routes were then changed to be as follows:

- 184 Malton, Firby, Leavening, Malton with two journeys on Tuesdays, Fridays and Saturdays.
- 185 Malton, Leavening, Westow, Kirkham to Firby with one journey on Tuesdays, Fridays and Saturdays.
- 186 Birdsall, Leavening, Harton, York on a Thursday with one journey.

Changes continued and operators changed, and from 10 May 2014, there were now journeys only on a Tuesday with no direct route to York.

To illustrate these changes further, from April 2016, a community-supported bus on a Tuesday started in Westow at 0907 as a 184 for Harton, Leppington, Acklam, Leavening, Burythorpe, Kennythorpe, Langton and Birdsall to Malton, arriving at 1030. The bus then performs as route 187, an 80-minute circular to villages off the A64 Scarborough road. At 1230, it goes on a two-hour circular 184 journey via Birdsall, Langton, Firby and Westow, from where it returns back, via the villages on the morning run, to Malton, arriving at 1430. The bus then becomes a 187 again leaving Malton at 1440 and returning at 1545. Finally, as a 185 it leaves Malton at 1630 for Birdsall, Langton, Kennythorpe, Burythorpe to Leavening, Leppington, Howsham, Westow, Kirkham to Firby, arriving at 1732.

Thus, changes to operators and reduced services have become the common pattern, especially for rural country routes and the former times of regular locally operated private and commercial services are now largely over outside cities and urban areas. The onus for running rural buses is now fully with local government and this means that when there are no successful tenders, or there is no community-supported service, services simply stop as, for example, has happened in Cumbria. Meanwhile, some local authorities, such as North Yorkshire, have chosen to run a small fleet of minibuses and operate services themselves.

Chapter 5

Gorwood Bros/Coaches

Here are 435BRB, on the route from Aughton, and SED232, from Thornton, parked up between runs on Foss Islands Road; each route had some joint lay over time at York. These two Bedford SBs were in the fleet together between 1967 and 1979. (Roy Marshall)

History

Gorwood was based in East Cottingwith. The company ran a horse bus in the late 1800s, which was not unusual in an agricultural farm environment, where horse power literally worked the fields, in a time when the wide use of the internal combustion engine was still in the future.

The generations of Garwoods involved in this small bus company were as follows:

- George, who was born in 1863, and his elder brother, William Reuben, born in 1859.
- William had four sons: George, born in 1890, Robert Pacey (always known as Perce), born in 1897, Leslie Charles, born in 1899, and Albert Stanley, born in 1902.
- Perce had a son, Ken, in May 1932, who went on to see the closing of bus activities.

The original horse-bus route was operated by William Reuben Gorwood and ran from Aughton, Ellerton, East Cottingwith, Sutton upon Derwent and Elvington to York. A single horse started from Aughton then, at East Cottingwith, a transfer took place to a bigger bus that was pulled by three horses. There is no record of how long the journey to York took. However, as the bus took one hour, a conservative estimate would be that it took around four or five hours by horse.

William's younger brother, George, also ran horse buses from Melbourne, three miles from East Cottingwith, but he ceased trading in 1923 or 1924 for health reasons and William then took over the route.

The initial company of Gorwood Brothers was formed in the early 1900s and became involved in the bus business in the early 1920s when William's sons, Leslie and Perce, joined the company. Brother Albert, meanwhile, was running a coal delivery business and George (Junior) was a full-time farmer. However, when needed, everyone helped on the farm. Indeed, George (Senior) thought being in the fields was work but driving a bus was not, it was 'just riding about'.

Whilst records do not seem to be complete, the first motor bus on the routes to York looks to have been a Crossley in 1921 followed by two new Ford buses in 1928 and 1929. The Fords lasted until the mid-1930s and were joined in 1930 by another Ford and in 1933 by a Chevrolet. In 1936, a new Bedford was bought and seems to have been the only bus at the time, along with perhaps the Chevrolet.

A second-hand Bedford came in 1942 and three further Bedfords were also bought second hand in 1942, 1945 and 1946. The 1945 purchase, said to have come from the Leicester area, was ex-War Department stock bought after Gorwood had failed, for the second time, to get a utility Bedford OWB allocated. These Bedfords were all gone between 1950 and 1952 and a second-hand Bedford OWB came in 1949 and then a new OB was purchased in 1950.

The fleet was at it maximum of five or six buses between 1948 and 1950. Exactly why this was the case is not known, although there would have been a post-war spike in demand. Whilst a military airfield was built nearby, at Melbourne, during the Second World War, Gorwood appears to have not been involved in any of the associated transport for this development. When they had tried, for the first time, to get a utility Bedford OWB allocated early in the Second World War, it was not allowed because of their low service bus mileage.

By the 1950s, the business was a regular 'lay-over attender' on Saturdays in York around Piccadilly/St Denys Road, along with Bailey of Fangfoss, Milburn of Leavening and Burley from Cawood, as well as, until 1953, Everingham from Pocklington. The relationship between Gorwood and Everingham was reported in the *Bus & Coach Buyer* (31 May 2002): 'there was something of a feud with Everingham, they wanted to see us gone, though we had been around longer.' Post-war, Everingham had wanted to run additional buses in front of both Gorwood and Bailey on the York Saturday market day services, and the application went before to the Traffic Commissioners in Leeds. Outside the Commissioners' offices comments were alleged to have been made by Everingham who stated that they wanted 'to get you of the road Perce', to which Perce Gorwood replied, 'we will still be here when you're gone'. Which actually turned out to be correct.

During the 1950s, more Bedford OBs were bought second hand and a new route was started once a week to Selby; this finished in 1960. The last OB came that year, after which Bedford SBs and, latterly, Bedford Y models, were used.

In February 1968, the daily service into York was sold off to East Yorkshire. Then, following Leslie's death in 1972, Ken became a partner with this father Perce. The Sunday York service was the next one to stop, the licence being surrendered in 1975.

When Perce Gorwood retired in 1974, Ken took over, and Perce died in December 1974. The business name was changed to Gorwood Coaches and the stage routes were later supplemented with three bus contracts and one car school contract. There were now three buses in the fleet but this grew to four in May 1975 when a Bedford YRQ with a Duple express body was added. This was purchased with the aid of a government new bus grant. Gorwood had been looking to buy another Bedford SB and had dispensation to do so under the grant scheme. However, it was delayed and because the dealers/coachbuilders Yeates had four Bedford YRQs in stock, Gorwood bought one of these.

The pattern of work was, by now, school work on weekdays and the York run on Saturdays. The buses were said to have never travelled more than 60 miles from East Cottingwith and, therefore, had a low mileage per bus; in 27 years the 1975 YRQ had only done 85,000 miles, had only needed routine maintenance and three water pumps and was only ever driven by Ken Gorwood.

Gorwood carried on operating the two Saturday services into York, probably because that is what they had always done. Ken Gorwood drove the route from passing his test at the age of 21 in 1953 until he was 67, and he only ever missed four trips in all of those years (two because he had mumps and the others because of friends' weddings). Ken also got married on a Wednesday and his three daughters were also married mid-week; family holidays were always taken nearby between Sunday and Friday.

However, in the late 1990s the service to York via Newton upon Derwent and Kexby Bridge was stopped, with the service via Elvington continuing and running twice a day on a Saturday.

Finally, in 1999, the stage bus routes were passed over to Thornes of Bubwith (and latterly, Hemingbrough) and the school contracts became Gorwood's main work along with some private hires. A later contract on a Thursday, running from East Cottingwith to Rossmoor, Melbourne, provided a connection with the East Yorkshire service 195 running between York and Pocklington.

The school contracts were continued using the three Bedfords (YRQ/SB5/YMT) and two part-time drivers. However, this work was finally given up when the contracts finished in July 2002. Ken Gorwood then retired and the business was closed.

However, as will be seen later, their preserved Bedford OB and SB buses had a life in East Cottingwith, at least for a few years.

Routes

The routes operated were as follows:

Service	From/to	Via	Days of operation and maximum trips	Journey time	Started/ finished
1	Aughton to York	Ellerton, East Cottingwith, Storwood, Hagg Bridge, Sutton upon Derwent, Elvington	Saturday 4 round trips	55/**60**/ 65 mins	Late 1800s / 2 January 1999 and passed to Thornes of Bubwith
2	Thornton to York	Melbourne, Ross Moor, Hagg Bridge, Sutton upon Derwent, Newton upon Derwent, Kexby Bridge	Saturday 3 round trips	50/**55**/ 65 mins	1923–24 / finished in the 1990s
3	Aughton to York	Ellerton, East Cottingwith, Storwood, Hagg Bridge, Sutton upon Derwent, Newton upon Derwent, Kexby Bridge.	Sunday 3 round trips	55 mins to York, 60 mins back	Licence not renewed in November 1975
4	Aughton to York	As service 3	3 journeys on Monday to Friday, 4 on Thursday and 1 on Saturday	**60**/65/ 70 mins	To EYMS in February 1968
5	Melbourne to Selby	East Cottingwith, Bubwith	Monday 1 round trip	Not known	1923–24 / finished in 1960 with licence surrendered June 1967

- The main journey time is in **bold**, whilst the other times suggest there were some untimetabled diversions.
- Some of the exact start dates remain unknown.
- The York terminus was originally the Queens Head Inn, 44 Fossgate, then sometime after 1954, St Denys Road, off Piccadilly.

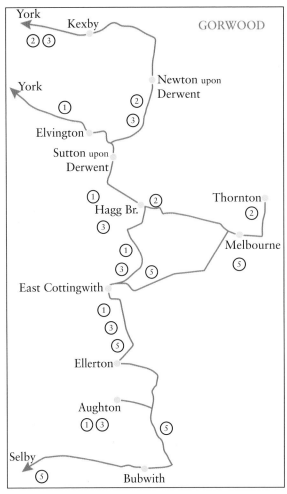

At the end, the Saturday Aughton to York route was operated by Gorwood with two Saturday round trips. When Thornes ran the service, they went on to introduce a York market Thursday service on a local authority contract (route 196). Also, they successfully tendered for the original Saturday service (route 195). Thornes badged these services as 'Gorwood Service' and the services were also extended from Aughton to Bubwith, a five-minute journey.

In 2000, Thornes improved the service quality with the introduction of a low-floor bus but then in 2007, as a result of spending cuts, East Riding of Yorkshire Council terminated the contracts. After lobbying by Thornes, the City of York Council, 'saved the service for a further 18 months' as 'the service was something of a lifeline for many regular elderly passengers, most of whom had already feared the ending of the facility with the demise of Garwood's' (Philip Thornes, 2019). After 18 months, when York Council announced the end of funding, East Riding Council put out a tender for the very same journeys to start when York Council withdrew. Thornes lost out on this and East Yorkshire MS took the service over on 1 May 2009.

Fleet
The fleet from 1950 is described and illustrated below.

Bedford OB/Duple Vista EVY44, with bus seats replacing the original coach seats and its winter radiator cover on, waits in Selby on Church Hill and looks to have had a bang on the driver's/emergency door. The Selby route from Melbourne had one journey on a Monday with an over five-hour 'park up' in Selby. EVY44 was Garwood's first new bus and cost £1,445 in April 1950. It was eventually fitted with a Perkins diesel engine and ran for 12 years, only requiring oil changes during that time. It worked until September 1967, after which is was scrapped. It was replaced by Bedford SB 435BRB. The Perkins engine was then re-bored and, with a new crankshaft, was put in LKH429. (Roy Marshall)

Another OB from 1946, HWJ621 was in the fleet from 1952 to 1957, when it was replaced by LKH429. No image has been traced of HWJ621. Above is OB FJW114, from 1948, in Selby. It came in January 1956 from Everall in Wolverhampton and stayed until September 1960 when it was replaced by OVF418. It possibly has a winged version of Garwood's garter fleet name. (Roy Marshall)

Bedford LKH429 was new in 1950 and came in October 1957 from Grey de Luxe in Hull. Again, seen on the lay over in Selby, it was withdrawn in October 1968 and keep for some years. For a time, it had the Perkins engine from EVY44 but later had a Bedford engine and was then fully preserved by Ken Gorwood. (Roy Marshall)

EF8983, from 1949, was the last OB seen in Selby before the route was withdrawn in 1960. It came in January 1960 from Welburn of nearby Snaith and is presumably still in their livery. It was withdrawn in March 1965 and replaced by SED232. (Roy Marshall)

OVF418, which replaced Bedford OB FJW114, is at Foss Islands Road, York, on lay over. It was new in 1953 and came from Babbage in Cromer in September 1960. It was a Bedford SB with a Yeates Rivera body and stayed until April 1972 when it was replaced by VCT547. Perce Gorwood is walking away and will no doubt be looking to meet up with the other bus from Thornton. (John Bennett)

Looking very smart on St Denys Road in York, SED232 is a 1958 Bedford SB3 with a Duple Vega body. New to Shadwell of Warrington, it came from Newtown in London WC1. It is seen here with a modified front grill with the chrome angel's wings missing, probably after accident damage. On this image, there is a gap in the trim above the number plate but on other images there is a patch.

It was a long-serving bus that had replaced Bedford OB EF8983 in April 1965 and stayed until July 1994. Its fuel consumption apparently went from 9 to 19mpg after fitting a Bedford 330 diesel engine. It was subsequently preserved by Ken Gorwood. (Peter Yeomans)

An earlier image of SED232 with its original 'butterfly' radiator and Duple Vega name lettering. (Peter Yeomans)

435BRB was a 1956 Bedford SBG with a Duple Vega body and came from Andrew, Tideswell, Derbyshire, in August 1967, replacing long-standing EVY44. Along with SED232, it was the mainstay of the fleet until its withdrawal in November 1979, when it was replaced by LRR152K. Withdrawn because of terminal fatigue of the window pillars, 435BRB eventually became derelict at the garage and is seen here parked higher up St Denys Road along with a Burley (trading as Majestic) bus. This is a 1964 Bedford SB5 with a Willowbrook bus body and was used on their daily route to Selby via Cawood. (Majestic will be fully covered in a book covering the western York independents.) (John Bennett)

Loading on St Denys Road is VCT547, which came in March 1972 and looks good with the small red flash. A Bedford SB5 with a Duple Super Vega body, it was new in May 1962 to Blankley of Colsterworth. It replaced OVF418 and stayed until the late 1970s when it was scrapped at the garage in East Cottingwith. (John Bennett)

KVY789N was a new bus grant-assisted purchase in May 1975. Waiting round the top corner of St Denys Road, it had run in off the route from Thornton via Melbourne and Newton. A Bedford YRQ with a Duple Dominant body, it stayed to the end and was passed to Thornes who placed it in their Heritage fleet in July 2002. They kept the Gorwood livery until 2013, when it was then painted into Thornes' own blue and grey livery. (Roy Marshall)

LRR152K was a 1972 Bedford SB5 with a Plaxton Panorama coach body, which was effectively the 1960s Embassy body that then became a Panorama when the Elite came in; coincidentally this version has the Elite II styled front. LRR152K came to Gorwood in November 1979 and replaced 435BRB.

As a larger vehicle was needed for a contract, in July 1994 a 1980 Bedford YMT with a Duple Dominant body was bought via Moseley dealers and re-registered as PIW4788. Originally, it had been with A. C. Coaches, London SE15, and was then registered as MMJ471V.

The Legacy
As mentioned, Ken Gorwood preserved two buses and these are illustrated below

Above and left: LKH429 is laid up at the farm after withdrawal. (Mike Davies)

LKH429 was passed to a private owner in 2006 and is seen here on show, possibly at Sandtoft Trolleybus Museum.

SED232 is on show (note the patch on the lower grill). **Ken Gorwood believes this was the best bus they ever had.** In 2002 he said: 'it has never been in any trouble, I drove it 50 miles a day on schools, more on a Thursday, 125 miles on service every Saturday and on private hire. None of the others ever did that much.' (Peter Henson)

Sold unroadworthy in September 2004 to Thornes, SED232 was re-registered as 696UXO. In October 2012, it was sold and was extensively overhauled at Ebor Trucks in York and brought back to PCV standards for Coastal & Country of Whitby to use on their local *Heartbeat* tours. From November 2016, it has been owned by Easton's Coaches, Stratton Strawless, Norfolk, and is seen here at Sheringham in July 2017.

That concludes our look at the independents running into York from the east and, as mentioned in the introduction, research never finishes as there are always gaps. Therefore, if anyone can assist to fill in such gaps, I would be delighted to hear from you. The follow-on book to this will cover the west side of York and will include operators such as Hopes, who ran from Malton, where they met Hutchinson and Reliance on routes into York, and Sykes and Burley/Majestic who ran in from the southwest.

References

Archives
The Bus Archive
Commercial Motor archive
Yorkshire Post archive

Books
Emmett, Stuart, *York Pullman, 1926 to 1985* (2018)
Jenkinson, Keith, *Twixt Wold, Carr and Coast: History of East Yorkshire Motor Services* (1992)
Motor Transport Yearbook 1937/38
Thornes, Philip, *The Coachman's Way* (2019)

Individuals
John Bennett, Matthew and Ian Gibbs, Charles Gill, David Marshall and Andy Sefton

Magazines and Newspapers
AEC Gazette, April 1939
Bus & Coach Buyer, 31 May 2002
Commercial Motor, 17 April 1942
The Omnibus Magazine, December 1957
Yorkshire Post and Leeds Intelligencer, 23 January 1938

Omnibus Society
Wright, John, *Independent Bus Services in the Yorkshire Traffic Area* (1979)
Lists of Independent Bus Services, July 1954

The PSV Circle Fleet Histories
East Yorkshire Motor Services Ltd, Part 1 (2018), reference PB33 (April 2018)
The Small Stage Carriage Operators of the Yorkshire Traffic Area Part 2, reference PB5 (October 1969)
York Pullman Bus Company Limited, reference PB26 (1992)

Websites
http://www.yorkshirefilmarchive.com/film/tower-pictorial-news-york-poor-childrens-fresh-air-fund-filey
http://www.leaveningonline.com/index.html
www.pocklingtonhistory.com
http://www.buslistsontheweb.co.uk/
http://lths.lutsociety.org.uk/index.html
http://www.old-bus-photos.co.uk/
http://www.sct61.org.uk/
https://issuu.com/bwhere/docs/evacuee_interviews